Juliet Falce-Robinson

University of California, Los Angeles

D1309292

Volume 1

Student Activities Manual

for

MOSAICOS

Spanish as a World Language

Fifth Edition

Matilde Olivella de Castells (Late)

Emerita, California State University, Los Angeles

Elizabeth E. Guzmán

University of Iowa

Paloma Lapuerta

Central Connecticut State University

Judith E. Liskin-Gasparro

University of Iowa

Prentice Hall
Upper Saddle River London Singapore Toronto
Tokyo Sydney Hong Kong Mexico City

Executive Editor: Julia Caballero
Development Editors: Elizabeth Lantz, Celia Meana
Executive Marketing Manager: Kris Ellis-Levy
Senior Marketing Manager: Denise Miller
Marketing Coordinator: William J. Bliss
Senior Managing Editor: Mary Rottino
Associate Managing Editor: Janice Stangel
Project Manager: Manuel Echevarria
Development Editor for Assessment: Melissa Marolla Brown
Media Editor: Meriel Martínez
Senior Media Editor: Samantha Alducin
Art Manager: Gail Cocker
Illustrator: Andrew Lange Illustration
Cartographer: Peter Bull Studio
Assistant Editor/EditorialCoordinator: Jennifer Murphy

Manufacturing Buyer: Cathleen Petersen
Manager, Print Production: Brian Mackey
Manager, Rights and Permissions: Zina Arabia
Manager, Visual Research: Beth Brenzel
Manager, Cover Visual Research & Permissions: Karen Sanatar
Image Permission Coordinator: Fran Toepfer
Photo Researcher: Diane Austin
Designer: Ximena Tamvakopoulos
Creative Design Director: Leslie Osher
Art Director, Interior: John Christiana
Editorial Assistant: Katie Spiegel
Publisher: Phil Miller
Composition/Full-Service Project Management: Macmillan Publishing Solutions
Printer/Binder: Bind-Rite Graphics

This book was set in 12/14 Sabon.

10 9 8 7 6 5 4

Prentice Hall is an imprint of

www.pearsonhighered.com

	Student Edition ISBN - 10:	0-205-66431-8
	ISBN - 13:	978-0-205-66431-3
	Volume 1 ISBN - 10:	0-205-68710-5
	ISBN - 13:	978-0-205-68710-7
	Volume 2 ISBN - 10:	0-205-68709-1
	ISBN - 13:	978-0-205-68709-1
	Volume 3 ISBN - 10:	0-205-68708-3
	ISBN - 13:	978-0-205-68708-4

CONTENTS

CAPÍTULO

PRELIMINAR

Bienvenidos

Nombre: _____

Fecha: _____

LAS PRESENTACIONES (TEXTBOOK P. 4)

P-1   María e Isabel. María and Isabel are meeting for the first time. Listen to María's statements and questions, and choose the most appropriate response for Isabel.

1. **a.** Mucho gusto.   **b.** Encantada.   **c.** Me llamo Isabel.

2. **a.** ¿Cómo te llamas?   **b.** Igualmente.   **c.** ¿Y tú?

3. **a.** ¿Y tú?   **b.** Mucho gusto.   **c.** Igualmente.

P-2   ¡Qué lío! Your best friend is recounting a Spanish conversation to you, but he has mixed everything up. Help your friend put the following sentences in order by numbering them correctly, 1–4.

Encantado, Adela. _____

Hola, me llamo Marina Camacho. ¿Cómo se llama usted? _____

Adela, mi amigo Carlos. _____

Me llamo Adela Pérez. _____

P-3   Presentaciones. Mary is spending a month in Zihuatanejo, Mexico. She has just met a few people, but her Spanish is not very good, so she does not know how to respond to them. Help Mary provide the appropriate responses.

1. CARLOS: Me llamo Carlos González, ¿y tú?

    MARY: _____

2. ROSA: Mary, mi amigo Juan.

    MARY: _____

3. ANABEL: Hola, ¿cómo te llamas?

    MARY: Me llamo Mary Jones.

    ANABEL: Mucho gusto.

    MARY: _____

LOS SALUDOS Y LAS DESPEDIDAS (TEXTBOOK P. 5-6)

P-4 Al teléfono. You work for a company in Mexico, answering phones and directing calls to the appropriate person. Write the greeting you would use at the following times of day.

1. 9:00 a.m. _____

2. 3:00 p.m. _____

3. 10:30 a.m. _____

4. 12:10 p.m. _____

5. 10:00 p.m. _____

6. 5:00 p.m. _____

P-5 ¡Ayuda! Mike has been invited to a party by a new friend. He knows that everyone at the party will be speaking Spanish. Choose the best response in each of the following situations.

1. Buenas noches, Mike.

    a. Buenas noches.   **b.** ¿Cómo está usted?   **c.** ¿Cómo estás?

2. Hola, Mike.

    a. ¿Qué tal?   **b.** Mucho gusto.   **c.** Igualmente.

3. Hola. ¿Cómo estás?

    a. Lo siento.   **b.** Bastante bien.   **c.** Gracias.

4. Hasta luego, Mike.

    a. Hola. ¿Qué tal?   **b.** Buenos días.   **c.** Adiós.

P-6 ¿Cómo están? Listen once to the conversation between Tomás, Pedro, and Ana to get the gist of it. Then listen again and fill in the blanks with the words you hear to describe how they are feeling. Finally, answer the two questions that follow.

TOMÁS: ¡Hola, Ana, Juan! ¿Qué tal?

ANA: (1)_____, ¿y tú?

TOMÁS: Bastante (2)_____.

PEDRO: Lo siento, Tomás.

TOMÁS: ¿Y cómo estas tú, Pedro?

PEDRO: Yo estoy (3)_____, gracias.

4. Who is feeling best? _____

5. Who is feeling worst? _____

EXPRESIONES DE CORTESÍA (TEXTBOOK P. 6-7)

P-7 Situaciones. It is important to be polite. Fill in the blanks for each situation below with the most appropriate Spanish expression from the word bank. One of the answers will be used twice.

con permiso   de nada   gracias   perdón   por favor

1. You apologize for spilling some coffee on your friend. _____

2. You ask your friend to lend you her class notes. _____

3. You ask your father to lend you money. _____

4. You say "you're welcome" after your mother thanks you for helping her.

_____

5. You are walking down the hallway and need to get your professor's attention.

_____

6. You thank your brother for lending you his car. _____

P-8 Cortesía. Listen to each statement and give the most appropriate response orally.

1. ...

2. ...

3. ...

4. ...

5. ...

P-9 Más expresiones. Tony is studying Spanish in Mexico City. He is going to have lunch before the afternoon classes start, and he encounters the situations below. Read each situation and fill in the blanks with the appropriate expression he could use in each case.

1. Tony is going out to lunch but will be coming back later. He says good-bye to his classmates. _____

2. Tony is trying to leave the classroom, but another student is blocking the door. Tony politely lets her know that he needs to move past her. _____

3. The student at the door moves aside and lets Tony walk out. Tony thanks her. _____

4. As he walks out, Tony bumps into his Spanish teacher. Tony apologizes. _____

5. He says good-bye to his teacher; they will see each other again tomorrow. _____

DISTINGUISHING REGISTERS (TEXTBOOK P. 7)

P-10 Formal o informal. As you already know, in Spanish there are formal and informal ways of introducing yourself and meeting people. Indicate whether the following introductions are formal or informal.

1. SRA. GÓMEZ: Buenos días, señor González.   formal
   SR. GONZÁLEZ: Buenos días, señora Gómez. ¿Cómo está usted?   informal
   SRA. GÓMEZ: Bien, gracias. ¿Y usted?
   SR. GONZÁLEZ: Bastante bien, gracias.

2. ROSA: Hola, ¿qué tal?   formal
   PEDRO: Regular.   informal
   ROSA: ¡Oh! Lo siento.

3. ISABEL: Hola, ¿cómo se llama?   formal
   CARLOS: Me llamo Carlos Aguirre, ¿y usted?   informal
   ISABEL: Soy Isabel Carrasco. Encantada.
   CARLOS: Igualmente.

4. JUANA: Marisol, mi amiga Inés.   formal
   MARISOL: Hola, Inés. Mucho gusto.   informal
   INÉS: Mucho gusto. ¿Cómo estás?
   MARISOL: Bien, gracias. ¿Y tú?
   INÉS: Muy bien, gracias.

P-11 **¿Formal o informal?** Listen to each of the introductions once and choose **formal** or **informal** to indicate how the speakers are addressing each other.

Conversación 1:   formal   informal

Conversación 2:   formal   informal

Conversación 3:   formal   informal

P-12 **¿Tú o usted?** Indicate the appropriate form of "you" that is used when speaking to the following people in Spanish.

1. la profesora   usted   tú

2. un amigo   usted   tú

3. un doctor   usted   tú

4. una chica   usted   tú

5. un estudiante   usted   tú

P-13 **¿Tú o usted?** Listen to the conversations, and then indicate in which conversation you hear the following.

1. tú   Conversación 1   Conversación 2

2. usted   Conversación 1   Conversación 2

3. ¿Qué tal?   Conversación 1   Conversación 2

4. ¿Cómo estás?   Conversación 1   Conversación 2

5. ¿Cómo está usted?   Conversación 1   Conversación 2

EL ALFABETO (TEXTBOOK P. 8)

P-14 **Nombres hispanos.** You and your friends are organizing a party, and you are in charge of calling six of the guests. Listen to your friend as he spells the first names of the six friends you have to call, and then choose the correct spelling of each name.

1. Beatris   Beatriz

2. Yolanda   Jolanda

3. Jorge   Gorge

4. Inaki   Iñaki

5. Joakín   Joaquín

6. Ignacio   Ignaxio

P-15   Más nombres hispanos. Do you recognize the names of these Hispanic celebrities? Listen to the spelling of each first and last name, and write it in the spaces provided. Be sure to use capital letters when necessary.

1. _____
2. _____
3. _____
4. _____

P-16   El mensaje. Two of your friends are on vacation in Cancún. You call the hotel and ask to speak with them. They are not in their room, so the receptionist asks you to leave a message. Spell their first and last names, as well as your own, orally for her.

MODELO: *Mi amiga se llama Katie Smith: k-a-t-i-e   s-m-i-t-h...*

IDENTIFICACIÓN Y DESCRIPCIÓN DE PERSONAS (TEXTBOOK P. 9)

P-17   ¿Cierto o falso? Felipe sees his friend Linda talking to a female student he does not know. He wants to find out more about her. Listen to Felipe's conversation with Linda and then indicate whether each statement is true (**Cierto**) or false (**Falso**).

1. Linda está muy mal.   Cierto   Falso
2. La amiga de Linda se llama Carmen.   Cierto   Falso
3. Carmen es amiga íntima de Felipe.   Cierto   Falso
4. Carmen es inteligente.   Cierto   Falso

P-18   ¿De qué habla? Read the descriptions Montserrat wrote and indicate to which person or object she is referring.

1. Es atractivo.
   a. el campus   **b.** los estudiantes   **c.** la chica
2. Eres valiente.
   a. yo   **b.** la profesora   **c.** tú
3. Soy responsable.
   a. el chico   **b.** yo   **c.** el estudiante
4. Es sentimental.
   a. tú   **b.** el actor   **c.** las profesoras

P-19   Sus opiniones. How would you describe the following people? Write a sentence for each, expressing your opinion. Remember to give the correct form of the adjective according to the gender of the subject, when necessary.

MODELO: El presidente de la universidad

El presidente de la universidad es responsable.

1. Jennifer López

_____

2. el estudiante

_____

3. mi amigo

_____

4. la profesora

_____

5. yo

_____

P-20   ¿Cómo son? Marcos's friend Teresa is giving a party (**una fiesta**), and Marcos invites Irene to come even though Irene does not know Teresa. Read Marcos's conversation with Irene and then indicate whether the statements that follow are **Cierto** or **Falso**.

MARCOS: Hola, Irene, ¿qué tal?

IRENE: Muy bien, ¿y tú?

MARCOS: Muy bien, gracias. Mi amiga Teresa va a (*is going to*) tener una fiesta. ¿Vienes? (*Are you coming?*)

IRENE: ¿Y cómo es Teresa?

MARCOS: Es muy interesante y popular.

IRENE: ¿Sí? Entonces es extrovertida.

VARCOS: Sí, y es muy dinámica y atractiva... pero tú eres dinámica y atractiva también (*too*).

IRENE: Gracias, Marcos.

1. Irene está bien.   Cierto   Falso

2. La amiga de Marcos se llama Teresa.   Cierto   Falso

3. Teresa es amiga íntima de Irene.   Cierto   Falso

4. Teresa es interesante y dinámica.   Cierto   Falso

5. Irene es atractiva.   Cierto   Falso

COGNADOS (TEXTBOOK P. 10)

P-21 ¿Cómo son Felipe y Carmen? Linda wants to arrange for Felipe and Carmen to meet because she thinks they are similar and would like each other. Listen to their conversation and select whether the following characteristics describe Carmen, Felipe, or both (**los dos**).

1. optimista   Felipe   Carmen   los dos
2. idealista   Felipe   Carmen   los dos
3. sentimental   Felipe   Carmen   los dos
4. realista   Felipe   Carmen   los dos
5. inteligente   Felipe   Carmen   los dos

P-22 Opuestos. Jorge and Luis are brothers, but they are complete opposites. Based on the adjectives used to describe Jorge, write the opposite word that describes what Luis is like.

introvertido   pasivo   serio

paciente   pesimista   tradicional

JORGE	LUIS
1. optimista	_____
2. liberal	_____
3. extrovertido	_____
4. activo	_____
5. cómico	_____
6. impaciente	_____

P-23 Los famosos. Decide whether the following statements are **Cierto** or **Falso**, according to what most people would say about these celebrities.

1. Eddie Murphy es introvertido y tímido.   Cierto   Falso
2. Ellen DeGeneres es cómica.   Cierto   Falso
3. Angelina Jolie es elegante.   Cierto   Falso
4. Steven Spielberg es creativo.   Cierto   Falso
5. Tiger Woods es atlético.   Cierto   Falso

P-24 **Cognados.** Because cognates can be helpful in understanding language, it is important to recognize them when you hear them. Listen to the following list of words, four of which are cognates. Write the cognates in the spaces provided in the order you hear them.

1. _____

2. _____

3. _____

4. _____

P-25 **Más cognados.** There are many English cognates in Spanish. Although these words are often easy to recognize when we see them, the pronunciation is different. Listen to each cognate and then read it out loud, being careful to imitate the Spanish pronunciation as closely as you can.

popular	perfeccionista	creativo
importante	eficiente	generoso
religioso	responsable	imparcial
serio	valiente	sincero
elegante	interesante	pasivo

¿QUÉ HAY EN EL SALÓN DE CLASE? (TEXTBOOK P. 11)

P-26 **En la clase.** In each of the following groups of items found in the classroom, select the item that does not belong.

1. mesa   borrador   pupitre   escritorio
2. computadora   televisor   grabadora   cesto
3. bolígrafo   lápiz   cuaderno   tiza
4. silla   pizarra   tiza   borrador
5. televisor   videocasetera   mochila   grabadora

P-27 **¿Qué tiene?** Identify the numbered items in Raúl's Spanish classroom.

1. _____   4. _____
2. _____   5. _____
3. _____

¿DÓNDE ESTÁ? (TEXTBOOK P. 12)

P-28 **¿Dónde está?** You will hear some statements about the location of several people and objects. Look at the illustration and then indicate if the statements are true (**Cierto**) or false (**Falso**).

1. Cierto   Falso   4. Cierto   Falso
2. Cierto   Falso   5. Cierto   Falso
3. Cierto   Falso   6. Cierto   Falso

P-29   El salón de clase. Think about your Spanish classroom and use the phrases below to indicate the usual location of the following objects and persons.

al lado de	detrás de	entre
debajo de	enfrente de	sobre

MODELO: el libro: *El libro está sobre la mesa.*

1. el profesor/la profesora: _____.

2. el cesto: _____.

3. la ventana: _____.

4. la pizarra: _____.

P-30   La clase de español. You are waiting for class to start and are explaining the location of people and objects to a friend. Write where the people and things are located in the classroom.

MODELO: La profesora: *La profesora está enfrente de la puerta.*

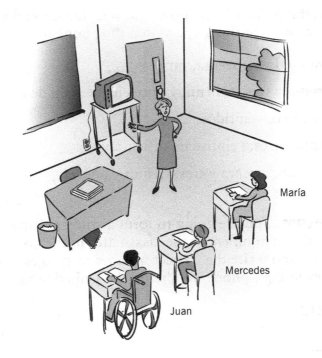

1. Mercedes: _____

2. el libro: _____

3. la pizarra: _____

4. el televisor: _____

5. María: _____

LISTENING WITH VISUALS (TEXTBOOK P. 13)

P-31   ¿Cómo se llaman? You already know all of your classmates' names except for four: three females and one male. Manuel, who is also in your class, has the seating chart. Listen to him to find out the names of the last four classmates. Then fill in the name of each one based on the information you hear.

Natalia	Pedro	Alberto	(1)_____
Rosa	Pablo	(2)_____	Irene
Carlos	Tomás	(3)_____	Federico
(4)_____	Marcela	Carmen	Manuel

LOS NÚMEROS 0 A 99 (TEXTBOOK P. 14-15)

P-32   Números de teléfono. You wrote down the telephone numbers of your classmates, but you may have mixed some of them up. Match the phone numbers with the right people.

1. Amanda: seis, sesenta y dos, noventa, quince ____

2. Alberto: ocho, cuarenta y tres, ochenta y uno, cincuenta y dos____

3. Luis: seis, ochenta y cinco, veintidós, trece____

4. Teresa: ocho, cuarenta y tres, veintisiete, ochenta y dos____

5. Marcos: cinco, dieciocho, sesenta y tres, treinta y nueve____

a. 843-2782

b. 685-2213

c. 518-6339

d. 662-9015

e. 843-8152

P-33   Agenda de teléfonos. You are going to form a study group for your chemistry class, so you write down the phone numbers of the classmates in the group. Listen to them as they say their phone numbers, and write the correct number next to each name. Be sure to write them as you would a seven-digit phone number in the United States.

MODELO: Luis: *477-2212*

1. Amelia: _____

2. Susana: _____

3. Mateo: _____

4. Beatriz: _____

5. David: _____

P-34   Problemas. Are you good at math? Solve the following problems, spelling out the answers. Be sure to follow the model exactly.

MODELO: 1 + 3 = *cuatro*

1. 10 + 1 = _____
2. 7 + 6 = _____
3. 35 − 12 = _____
4. 99 − 22 = _____

5. 50 − 15 = _____
6. 20 + 2 = _____
7. 15 + 21 = _____
8. 48 − 2 = _____

P-35   Bingo. You are playing Bingo with your friends at the Spanish Club. Listen to the numbers and write them in the spaces provided. Then check your card for matches: if you have the whole card, write **bingo**, if you have a line write **línea**, or if you have nothing, write **nada**.

1. _____
2. _____
3. _____
4. _____
5. _____
6. _____
7. _____
8. _____

B	I	N	G	O
5	16	31	48	62
8	18	38	50	65
10	21	FREE SPACE	55	68
13	22	42	56	70
15	30	45	60	75

9. ¿Bingo, línea o nada? _____

LOS MESES DEL AÑO Y LOS DÍAS DE LA SEMANA (TEXTBOOK P. 16-17)

P-36   Los días de la semana. Write in Spanish the day of the week that best corresponds to each statement.

1. This is the first day of the weekend. _____

2. This is the first day of the week on calendars in most Hispanic countries. _____

3. This is the last day of the week on calendars in most Hispanic countries. _____

4. Thanksgiving is traditionally celebrated on this day of the week. _____

5. When the 13th falls on this day, some in the United States consider it bad luck. _____

P-37   Los meses. Think of the holidays on the United States calendar, and match each holiday with the appropriate month.

1. el Día del Trabajo (*Labor Day*)___   **a.** julio

2. el Día de Año Nuevo (*New Year's Day*)____   **b.** septiembre

3. el Día de San Patricio (*Saint Patrick's Day*)____   **c.** diciembre

4. el Día de Acción de Gracias (*Thanksgiving*)____   **d.** febrero

5. el Día de la Raza (*Columbus Day*)____   **e.** enero

6. el Día de la Independencia____   **f.** noviembre

7. el Día de Navidad (*Christmas*)____   **g.** octubre

8. el Día de los Presidentes____   **h.** marzo

P-38   Días y meses. Mark is starting to learn Spanish and he is trying to clarify some things about the names of the days of the week and the months. Help him out by selecting whether what he is saying is correct (**Sí**) or incorrect (**No**).

1. Sí   No

2. Sí   No

3. Sí   No

4. Sí   No

5. Sí   No

P-39 Más días y meses. Mark is still having some trouble remembering the days of the week and the months in Spanish. He keeps forgetting two days and three months. Listen to him and write the days and the months he is forgetting in the spaces provided and in chronological order.

Días de la semana: **1.** _____   **2.** _____

Meses del año: **3.** _____   **4.** _____   **5.** _____

P-40 ¿Qué día es? Look at the calendar. You will be asked on what days of the week certain dates fall. Answer each question by writing the appropriate day.

Octubre						
L	M	M	J	V	S	D
			1	2	3	4
5	6	7	8	9	10	11
12	13	14	15	16	17	18
19	20	21	22	23	24	25
26	27	28	29	30	31	

MODELO: You hear: ¿Qué día es el 10?
You write: *sábado*

1. _____   **5.** _____

2. _____   **6.** _____

3. _____   **7.** _____

4. _____

P-41 Secuencias. Look at the following sequences and complete them with the most appropriate day or month.

1. lunes, martes, _____

2. octubre, noviembre, _____

3. viernes, _____, domingo

4. junio, julio, _____

5. febrero, _____, abril

6. miércoles, _____, viernes

7. domingo, lunes, _____

8. noviembre, diciembre, _____

LA HORA (TEXTBOOK P. 18)

P-42   ¿Qué hora es? You will hear a time for each clock you see. If the time you hear corresponds to the time shown on the clock, select **Sí**. If it does not correspond, select **No**.

1. `oo| 9:00 |`   Sí   No
2. `oo| 4:10 |`   Sí   No
3. `oo| 10:30 |`   Sí   No
4. `oo| 2:15 |`   Sí   No
5. `oo| 6:50 |`   Sí   No

P-43   La hora del tren. Your friend Cara is traveling in Spain and has asked you to pick her up at the station today. You know that she is arriving at 8:50 p.m., but you are unsure where she is coming from. Listen to the arrival times (**llega** = *arrives*) for tonight and write them down in digits. Finally, write the name of the city she is coming from in the last space.

1. Málaga: _____
2. Barcelona: _____
3. Valencia: _____
4. Sevilla: _____
5. Toledo: _____
6. Cara llega de: _____

P-44   ¿A qué hora sale el autobús? Cara is already planning her next trip, and she decides she will go wherever the earliest bus takes her. You call the station for her and listen to tomorrow's departure schedule. Write the departure time (**sale** = *departs*) in digits next to each city. Finally, write the name of the city she is going to in the last space.

1. Málaga: _____
2. Barcelona: _____
3. Madrid: _____
4. Valencia: _____
5. Toledo: _____
6. Cara sale para (*for*): _____

P-45 Las clases. María and Susana have to take the same classes this semester. Susana does not get along with María and does not want to take any classes at the same time as her. Below are the possible class schedule and María's schedule. At what times does Susana have to take her classes to avoid María? Spell out the appropriate times, and remember to indicate morning (**de la mañana**) or afternoon (**de la tarde**).

Horario de clases:

ESPAÑOL	COMUNICACIÓN	HISTORIA	LITERATURA	INGLÉS	MATEMÁTICAS
Sección 1 9:30 a.m.	Sección 1 11:00 a.m.	Sección 1 12:30 p.m.	Sección 1 9:30 a.m.	Sección 1 10:40 a.m.	Sección 1 10:20 a.m.
Sección 2 1:00 a.m.	Sección 2 2:30 p.m.	Sección 2 4:45 p.m.	Sección 2 11:00 a.m.	Sección 2 2:15 p.m.	Sección 2 1:15 p.m.

Clases de María:

Español, Sección 2   Historia, Sección 1   Comunicación, Sección 1

Literatura, Sección 1   Inglés, Sección 2   Matemáticas, Sección 2

Clases de Susana:

MODELO: hora de la clase de matemáticas: *las diez y veinte de la mañana*

1. hora de la clase de español: _____

2. hora de la clase de historia: _____

3. hora de la clase de literatura: _____

4. hora de la clase de comunicación: _____

5. hora de la clase de inglés: _____

P-46 Una graduación. Your brother has received an invitation to his friend's graduation from medical school, but he is not at home to open it. When he calls, you tell him about the invitation and he asks you to give him the information. Fill in the blanks with the correct answers.

> *El Presidente y Decano, La Facultad*
> *y la Clase Graduada de la*
> *Escuela Superior de Medicina de Ponce*
> *tienen el placer de invitarle a la*
> *Ceremonia de Graduación*
> *que se celebrará el*
> *Sábado, 26 de mayo de 2005*
> *a las 10:00 de la mañana*
> *en el Teatro La Perla (Ponce)*
> *Le seguirá recepción*
> *a las 11:45 de la mañana*

1. El día de la graduación es _____.

2. El mes de la graduación es _____.

3. La ceremonia es a las _____ de la _____.

4. La recepción es a las _____ de la _____.

5. La ceremonia es en _____.

EL TIEMPO (TEXTBOOK P. 19)

P-47 ¿Qué tiempo hace hoy? Write a complete sentence that describes the weather in each of the pictures.

1.

2.

3.

1. _____.

2. _____.

3. _____.

P-48   Las vacaciones. You and your roommate are looking ahead to your next vacation, and you want to choose a destination with nice weather during the months you plan to go. Write complete sentences to describe the typical weather in the following cities.

1. San Diego, California en junio:

_____

2. Phoenix, Arizona en julio:

_____

3. New York City en enero:

_____

4. Seattle, Washington en abril:

_____

5. Boston, Massachusetts en octubre:

_____

EXPRESIONES ÚTILES EN LA CLASE (TEXTBOOK P. 20)

P-49   ¿Quién lo dice? Indicate who would be most likely to make the following statements in a Spanish classroom: a student (**estudiante**) or the instructor (**profesor**).

1. ¿Comprenden?   estudiante   profesor

2. ¿En qué página?   estudiante   profesor

3. ¿Tienen alguna pregunta?   estudiante   profesor

4. Más despacio, por favor.   estudiante   profesor

5. Tengo una pregunta.   estudiante   profesor

6. Presente.   estudiante   profesor

P-50   En la clase. You will hear several expressions that are frequently used in class. Write in the space provided the letter of the expression that describes each illustration.

1. _____   2. _____   3. _____   4. _____

P-51   ¿Qué dice usted? This is your first semester taking Spanish, and you will have to speak in Spanish in class. In the following situations, indicate what you would say.

1. You want the professor to repeat something he/she just said. _____.

2. You ask your classmate to speak more loudly. _____.

3. You do not understand something. _____.

4. You do not know the answer. _____.

P-52   ¡Escuche! You will hear some additional classroom expressions. Select the English equivalent for each one.

1. **a.** The homework, please.   **b.** Again, please.

2. **a.** Raise your hand.   **b.** Answer.

3. **a.** Answer.   **b.** Repeat.

4. **a.** Read.   **b.** Write.

1

Nombre: _____

Fecha: _____

En la universidad

A PRIMERA VISTA

1-1   Mi vida de estudiante. Daniel is an American student in a study abroad program in Spain. Today, in his first Spanish class, he is introducing himself to his classmates. Read the following statements, listen to Daniel and finally indicate whether each statement is true (**Cierto**) or false (**Falso**).

1. Daniel estudia en la Universidad de Salamanca.   Cierto   Falso

2. Daniel no trabaja.   Cierto   Falso

3. Daniel estudia matemáticas y psicología.   Cierto   Falso

4. La clase de estadística es fácil.   Cierto   Falso

5. Daniel saca malas notas en estadística.   Cierto   Falso

6. La profesora de español es buena.   Cierto   Falso

7. Daniel practica español en la oficina.   Cierto   Falso

8. Daniel trabaja con personas norteamericanas.   Cierto   Falso

1-2 El horario de clases. Chris, another study abroad student at the Universidad Complutense in Madrid, is describing the courses he is taking this semester. Match each course with the correct description.

_____ 1. Esta clase es difícil. Practico mucho con la computadora.

_____ 2. En esta clase aprendemos sobre (*we learn about*) los eventos del pasado (*the past*).

_____ 3. Esta es mi clase favorita. Trabajo con un mapa y aprendo sobre las realidades geofísicas del planeta.

_____ 4. En esta clase hablamos sobre el estado mental de las personas.

_____ 5. En esta clase necesito un diccionario a veces. También aprendo mucho vocabulario y gramática.

a. informática

b. geografía

c. historia

d. español

e. psicología

1-3 Una conversación con Andrea. Daniel has met Andrea in their biology class, and is curious about her, so he asks a lot of questions. Listen to their conversation and then complete Andrea's answers with the correct information.

1. La clase de _____ es mi favorita.

2. Sí, trabajo en una _____.

3. Tomo _____, literatura y economía.

4. No, todas mis clases son _____.

5. La clase de historia es muy _____.

6. Estudio para los exámenes en la _____.

1-4 El alumno nuevo. Miguel, a new student, is telling Daniel about some of his classes, but he is a little confused. Read Miguel's statements and determine whether they are **Cierto** or **Falso**.

1. En la clase de historia hablamos de los presidentes como Abraham Lincoln y de otra gente importante como Susan B. Anthony.   Cierto   Falso

2. En la clase de literatura tocamos el piano y la guitarra.   Cierto   Falso

3. Todos los días en la clase de estadística necesito un mapa del mundo (*world*).   Cierto   Falso

4. A veces en la clase de economía necesitamos una calculadora.   Cierto   Falso

5. En la clase de informática usamos las computadoras.   Cierto   Falso

1-5   ¿Similar o diferente? Daniel has now spent a few weeks in Spain, and he has learned some things about college life. Listen to him talk about some of the differences between college life in the United States and in Spain. Finally, answer the questions with the information you hear.

	ESTUDIANTES EN ESTADOS UNIDOS	ESTUDIANTES EN ESPAÑA
¿Trabajan y estudian?	Sí	(1)
¿Qué hacen por las tardes?	Van al gimnasio.	Van a la plaza.
¿Qué deporte practican?	(2)	Fútbol
¿Dónde estudian?	(3)	(4)
¿Dónde toman algo por la noche?	(5)	(6)

1-6   Su horario. It is important to be organized. Write down your schedule for this semester, indicating the time, day, and name of each class.

HORA	DÍA	CLASE
_____	_____	_____
_____	_____	_____
_____	_____	_____
_____	_____	_____
_____	_____	_____

Nombre: _____   Fecha: _____

1-7 ¿Qué opina usted? Indicate your opinion about the following, using the correct forms of the verb **ser** and the adjectives provided. Be sure to make the adjectives agree with the subjects given in number and gender.

aburrido/a	difícil	fácil	interesante	pequeño/a
bueno/a	excelente	grande	malo/a	regular

MODELO: mi clase de español:

Mi clase de español es divertida.

1. mis clases: _____

2. mis amigos: _____

3. mi casa: _____

4. montar en bicicleta: _____

5. bailar salsa: _____

6. las telenovelas (*soap operas*): _____

7. hablar por teléfono: _____

8. el cine: _____

9. la cafetería de la universidad: _____

10. la playa: _____

1-8 Las actividades de los estudiantes. Daniel is getting to know the different places around campus. Match each activity listed below with the place in which it is usually done.

_____ 1. estudiar   **a.** el laboratorio de lenguas

_____ 2. tomar apuntes   **b.** el gimnasio

_____ 3. hacer ejercicio   **c.** la librería

_____ 4. comer   **d.** la cafetería

_____ 5. comprar libros   **e.** la biblioteca

_____ 6. practicar español **f.** la clase

1-9   La universidad. Find the following words related to student life in the puzzle below. Be sure to look for words horizontally, vertically, and diagonally.

| alumno | biblioteca | gimnasio | libro | notas | tarea |

t	e	b	g	i	m	n	a	s	i	o
a	a	a	r	m	i	e	s	t	l	e
o	i	r	a	n	o	i	c	c	i	d
b	l	e	e	s	t	c	a	s	e	l
i	c	e	a	a	g	o	a	f	m	e
b	t	i	d	m	n	t	u	i	f	r
l	h	i	o	c	o	j	i	a	l	a
i	c	a	r	n	s	o	a	m	r	a
o	ñ	e	a	l	i	b	r	o	r	s
t	u	a	d	e	r	n	p	c	o	n
e	u	n	i	v	e	r	o	l	a	p
c	a	l	u	m	n	o	d	o	r	a
a	f	i	l	o	s	o	g	o	n	a

1-10   Su clase favorita. Write a brief paragraph in Spanish describing your favorite class. Remember to include the following information:

- the name of the class
- the day and time of the class
- whether the class is easy, difficult, interesting, or boring
- whether you have a lot of homework
- whether you get good grades

_____

_____

_____

_____

_____

_____

EN ACCIÓN

1-11   Antes de ver. In this video segment, you are introduced to the main character, Javier, who is traveling from Colombia to México. Make a list of some of the countries that he might pass on his way.

_____

_____

_____

_____

_____

1-12   Mientras ve. As you watch the video, indicate whether the following statements are true (**Cierto**), false (**Falso**), or the information is not provided (**No dice**).

1. Javier es colombiano.
   Cierto   Falso   No dice

2. Javier no tiene amigos en México.
   Cierto   Falso   No dice

3. Daniel estudia mucho.
   Cierto   Falso   No dice

4. Daniel tiene clases de álgebra y física.
   Cierto   Falso   No dice

5. A Gabi le gustan las artes y el baile.
   Cierto   Falso   No dice

6. El teléfono de Gabi está en la cafetería.
   Cierto   Falso   No dice

7. La bicicleta es de Daniel.
   Cierto   Falso   No dice

1-13.   Después de ver. Do you remember what the characters are like? Write one word that describes each of them.

cómico   simpática   puntual

1. Daniel: _____   **2.** Javier: _____   **3.** Gabi: _____

FUNCIONES Y FORMAS

1. Talking about academic life and daily occurrences: Present tense of regular -ar verbs (Textbook p. 32)

1-14   Un día típico. Luis is one of Daniel's professors in Madrid, and many of his daily activities are similar to those of his students. Read the list of activities below, and then listen to Luis. Finally, select **Sí** if Luis mentions the activity, and **No** if he does not.

1. tomar café	Sí No
2. estudiar en la biblioteca	Sí No
3. bailar en la discoteca	Sí No
4. trabajar en la oficina	Sí No
5. revisar las tareas de los estudiantes	Sí No
6. caminar a casa	Sí No
7. montar en bicicleta	Sí No
8. practicar el piano	Sí No

1-15   ¿Quién? Daniel, Andrea, and their friends have a very busy life. Read the following sentences and write the correct subject pronoun to indicate who does each of the activities.

MODELO: Usamos un diccionario en la clase.   *nosotros o nosotras*

1. Practica español en clase. _____
2. Escucho música rock. _____
3. Compran libros para (*for*) la clase de literatura americana. _____
4. Conversas por teléfono. _____
5. Preparamos la cena en el apartamento. _____
6. Miro la televisión por la noche. _____
7. Estudias en la biblioteca. _____
8. Habla con su novia todos los días. _____
9. Trabajan en un restaurante. _____

1-16   Andrea. Andrea is a typical student. Complete the sentences that describe her with the correct forms of the verbs in parentheses.

1. Andrea _____ (llegar) a la universidad a las ocho de la mañana.
2. Todos los días _____ (estudiar) en la biblioteca.

3. En clase, siempre _____ (escuchar) al profesor.

4. Todos los días _____ (trabajar) por la tarde.

5. Muchas veces _____ (mirar) la televisión por la noche.

6. Los fines de semana _____ (bailar) en una discoteca.

1-17   La vida de los estudiantes. Complete the following paragraph with the correct verb forms, to indicate the typical activities you and your friends do at the university.

En la universidad, mis amigos y yo (1)_____ en la biblioteca. Mi amiga (2)_____ después de las clases. Mis amigos también (3)_____ en la discoteca los sábados por la noche. Uno de ellos (4)_____ buenas notas en sus clases. Por la noche, él (5)_____ café en la cafetería de la universidad, pero yo (6)_____ la televisión. Mis amigos y yo (7)_____ el piano los fines de semana.

1-18   Un día típico en tu vida. Explain orally the things you do on a typical day, and be sure to include at least three different activities from the lists below.

bailar	estudiar	montar
caminar	hablar	tomar
comprar	llegar	practicar
escuchar	mirar	trabajar

2. Talking about academic life and daily occurrences: Present tense of regular -er and -ir verbs (Textbook p. 36)

1-19   ¿Qué hacen? Daniel tells Andrea that he and his friend study a lot, but that they also do other things everyday. Read the following sentence fragments and fill in the correct subject or subject pronoun based on the verb forms given.

| Yo   Nosotros   Chris   Mis amigos   Tú |

1. _____ lee el periódico.

2. _____ bebes café.

3. _____ aprendemos español.

4. _____ asisten a clase.

5. _____ como en la cafetería.

1-20 ¿Estudiante o profesor? Students' and professors' activities are often similar. Listen to a student and a professor talk about their daily activities. Then select whether each statement below refers to the student, the professor, or both (**los dos**).

1. Mira la televisión.   estudiante   profesor   los dos
2. Aprende inglés.   estudiante   profesor   los dos
3. Lee libros de detectives.   estudiante   profesor   los dos
4. Come en la cafetería de la universidad.   estudiante   profesor   los dos
5. Monta en bicicleta los fines de semana.   estudiante   profesor   los dos
6. Llega a la universidad por la tarde.   estudiante   profesor   los dos
7. Asiste a conferencias sobre biología.   estudiante   profesor   los dos
8. Escribe composiciones.   estudiante   profesor   los dos

1-21 Mis amigos. Daniel has made a lot of new friends during his study abroad experience. Complete his description with the appropriate forms of the verbs in parentheses.

Mis amigos y yo (1) _____ (vivir) en un apartamento. Somos cuatro personas. Yo (2) _____ (estudiar) español. Mi amigo Raúl (3) _____ (estudiar) biología, y Carlos y Javier (4) _____ (estudiar) medicina. Por la mañana, yo (5) _____ (preparar) café y todos nosotros (6) _____ (desayunar). Más tarde, nosotros (7) _____ (asistir) a clase. A veces, yo (8) _____ (leer) en la biblioteca después de clase. Raúl y Javier (9) _____ (trabajar) después de las clases. Normalmente, ellos (10) _____ (comer) en la cafetería. Carlos y yo (11) _____ (comer) en casa. Por la noche, mis amigos y yo (12) _____ (escribir) la tarea. Los viernes por la noche todos nosotros (13) _____ (comer) pizza, y los sábados (14) _____ (asistir) a una fiesta. ¡Me encanta la vida estudiantil!

1-22 ¿Los conoce bien? Think of your friends and family members. Do you know their routines? For each of the following people, write three sentences describing a typical day. Use at least three different verbs from the word bank for each.

aprender	comer	escribir	hablar	practicar
asistir	comprar	estudiar	leer	vivir

su mejor amigo:

1. _____
2. _____
3. _____

sus padres:

1. _____

2. _____

3. _____

usted:

1. _____

2. _____

3. _____

3. Specifying gender and number: Articles and nouns (Textbook p. 39)

1-23   En la universidad. Below are some people, places, and objects you can find in a university. Fill in the appropriate definite article: **el, la, los, las.**

1. _____ cuadernos

2. _____ mapa

3. _____ sillas

4. _____ tarea

5. _____ libro

6. _____ mesas

7. _____ compañera

8. _____ laboratorios

1-24   Horas de oficina. Andrea is having some trouble with her economics class, so she wants to ask her instructor a few questions during his office hours. She talks to his secretary, señor Marín. Read the conversation carefully and fill in the spaces with **el, la, los, las,** or **X** if no article is needed.

ANDREA: Buenos días, (1) _____ señor Marín. ¿Está (2) _____ señor Torres en (3) _____ oficina?

SR. MARÍN: No, no está en este momento.

ANDREA: Ah... y, ¿cuándo tiene horas de oficina (4) _____ señor Torres?

SR. MARÍN: Todos (5) _____ días, a (6) _____ 10:30 de la mañana.

ANDREA: ¡Gracias, (7) _____ señor Marín!

1-25   **¡Yo tengo dos!** For everything Daniel has, Andrea has two. Listen to what Daniel says, and then write Andrea's response. Be sure to follow the model exactly.

MODELO: You hear: Yo tengo un bolígrafo.

   You write: *Yo tengo dos bolígrafos.*

1. _____

2. _____

3. _____

4. _____

5. _____

1-26   **¿Qué necesita?** Each of these people wishes to do (**quiere** + *infinitive*) several activities, but lack the things they need. Using the correct form of **necesitar**, write the item or place that they need to complete their tasks. Remember to include the appropriate indefinite article: **un, una, unos, unas.**

bolígrafo	diccionario	librería	televisor
calculadora	discoteca	mapa	

MODELO: Diana quiere estudiar literatura.   *Necesita un libro.*

1. Carlos quiere tomar apuntes. _____

2. Luis y Javier quieren buscar el significado (*meaning*) de "escritorio".

   _____

3. Raúl quiere practicar las matemáticas. _____

4. Emilia quiere comprar un lápiz. _____

5. Tú quieres bailar salsa. _____

6. Yo quiero buscar las naciones que limitan (*border*) con Colombia.

   _____

7. Chris quiere mirar el programa *American Idol.* _____

1-27   De compras. Now Andrea is helping Chris shop for school supplies. Read Chris's shopping list and tell Andrea orally the number of items he needs.

MODELO: You see: libro (6)

You say: *Necesita seis libros.*

1. lápiz (5)
2. bolígrafo (5)
3. mochila (2)
4. cuaderno (4)
5. mapa (3)

6. calculadora (2)
7. CD (6)
8. papel (25)
9. libro (8)
10. computadora (1)

1-28   ¿Qué necesito comprar? Write a brief paragraph listing all the supplies you need in order to do well in your classes. Remember to include the appropriate indefinite articles: **un, una, unos, unas.**

_____

_____

_____

_____

_____

_____

_____

4. Expressing location and states of being: Present tense of *estar* (Textbook p. 42)

1-29   Una cita. Andrea calls her friend Jaime on his cell phone to see if he wants to meet up with her. Complete their conversation with the correct form of **estar**.

ANDREA: Hola, Jaime, soy Andrea. ¿Cómo (1) _____?

JAIME: Hola, Andrea. (2) _____ muy bien, ¿y tú?

ANDREA: Yo, bien, gracias. ¿Dónde (3) _____ ahora (*now*)?

JAIME: (4) _____ en casa, y miro la televisión. ¿Y tú?

ANDREA: (5) _____ en la universidad.

JAIME: ¿Daniel (6) _____ en la universidad también (*too*)?

ANDREA: No, él (7) _____ en la oficina, pero llega a las tres. ¿Quieres venir?

JAIME: Sí. ¿Las 3:30 es una buena hora? Generalmente, ¿dónde (8) _____ ustedes a las 3:30?

ANDREA: A las 3:30 Daniel y yo (9) _____ en la cafetería.

JAIME: Perfecto. Hasta entonces (*Until then*).

1-30   ¿Dónde están? Consider what the following people are doing, and use the phrases below to indicate where they are. Be sure to use the correct form of **estar**.

en la biblioteca	en el gimnasio	en el restaurante
en la discoteca	en la librería	

MODELO: Javier nada.   *Está en la playa.*

1. Daniel estudia. _____

2. Andrea baila. _____

3. Chris y Daniel comen. _____

4. Andrea y Marisa practican gimnasia aeróbica. _____

5. Carlos y yo compramos un libro. _____

1-31 ¿**Cuándo tomamos un café?** You and some of your classmates want to meet for a Spanish conversation hour on Tuesdays, but you all have busy schedules. Listen to your classmates tell you about their activities for Tuesday, and complete the following agenda. Be sure to include the subject or subject pronoun in your answer, as in the model, and for the times that are vacant, write an **X** in the space. Finally, answer the last question.

MARTES	
9:00	*Yo estoy en la clase de matemáticas.*
10:00	(1) _____
11:00	(2) _____
12:00	(3) _____
1:00	(4) _____
2:00	(5) _____
3:00	(6) _____

7. Podemos reunirnos (*we can meet*) a las _____ o a la _____.

1-32 **Su rutina y la de sus amigos.** Write sentences describing where you and your friends are at the following times. Remember to write out the times in words.

MODELO: Usted, el miércoles a las 8:00 de la mañana:

A las ocho de la mañana, estoy en el gimnasio.

1. su mejor amiga, el lunes a las 3:30 de la tarde:

_____

2. Usted, el domingo a las 10:00 de la mañana:

_____

3. su madre, el martes a las 4:00 de la tarde:

_____

4. Usted, el miércoles a las 7:00 de la tarde:

_____

5. Su compañero/a de cuarto (*roommate*) y usted, el sábado a las 9:00 de la noche:

_____

1-33   ¿Dónde está la biblioteca? Your Spanish conversation group is going to have its first meeting at the library, but you do not know where the library is! As you listen to your friend María give directions, look at the campus map and label the names of the buildings she describes until you find the library. Finally, make note of exactly where the library is.

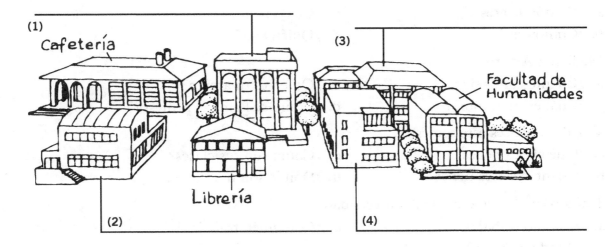

(1) Cafetería

(3)

Facultad de Humanidades

Librería

(2)

(4)

5. La biblioteca está entre _____ y _____.

5. Asking and answering questions: Interrogative words (Textbook p. 44)

1-34   En orden. Last week your Spanish teacher asked you to interview a Spanish friend for homework. You interviewed your friend Carlos about his studies and recorded his answers, but you realized you did not ask the questions in the order you had written them. Listen to the recording and match the appropriate answer with the corresponding question.

1. Tú eres español, ¿verdad?   _____

2. ¿Dónde estudias?   _____

3. ¿Por qué estudias allí?   _____

4. ¿Cuántas clases tomas?   _____

5. ¿Qué clases tomas?   _____

6. ¿Cuál es tu clase favorita?   _____

7. ¿Cómo es el profesor de esa clase?   _____

8. ¿Estudias inglés?   _____

1-35   Interferencias. You are listening to an interview of an exchange student from Spain on the university radio station. However, there is a lot of static and you cannot hear the interviewer very well. Choose the question that prompted each response.

1. Soy de Madrid.
   a. ¿De dónde eres?
   b. ¿Cómo eres?
   c. ¿Cuál eres?
   d. ¿Quién eres?

2. Me llamo Arturo.
   a. ¿Cuántos años tienes?
   b. ¿Cuál es tu nombre?
   c. ¿Quién es tu amigo?
   d. ¿Cómo se llama el profesor?

3. Tengo seis clases este semestre.
   a. ¿Qué clases tienes?
   b. ¿Cuántas clases tienes?
   c. ¿Cómo son tus clases?
   d. ¿Dónde son tus clases?

4. Trabajo en el periódico de la universidad.
   a. ¿Cuándo trabajas?
   b. ¿Dónde trabajas?
   c. ¿Con quién trabajas?
   d. ¿Cuánto trabajas?

5. Porque quiero aprender sobre la cultura americana.
   a. ¿Con quién estás en Estados Unidos?
   b. ¿Por qué estás en Estados Unidos?
   c. ¿Dónde estás en Estados Unidos?
   d. ¿Por cuánto tiempo estás en Estados Unidos?

6. Soy inteligente y divertido.
   a. ¿Qué eres?
   b. ¿Quién eres?
   c. ¿Cómo eres?
   d. ¿Cuál eres?

7. Estoy en Estados Unidos por un año.
   a. ¿Cuándo llegas a Estados Unidos?
   b. ¿Por qué estás en Estados Unidos?
   c. ¿Dónde estás en Estados Unidos?
   d. ¿Cuánto tiempo estás en Estados Unidos?

8. Estudio en la residencia estudiantil.
   a. ¿Con quién estudias?
   b. ¿Cómo estudias?
   c. ¿Dónde estudias?
   d. ¿Por qué estudias en la residencia?

1-36   La universidad. You just returned home from the university, and your brother, a senior in high school, wants to know everything about your life there. Complete his questions with the appropriate interrogative word.

1. —¿ _____ son los profesores? —Los profesores son muy inteligentes.

   Cómo   Cuándo   Qué   Dónde

2. —¿ _____ es tu clase favorita? —Mi clase favorita es español.

   Qué   Cómo   Por qué   Cuál

3. —¿ _____ amigos tienes? —Tengo muchos amigos.

   Quiénes   Cuántos   Dónde   Cuáles

4. —¿ _____ comes? —Como en la cafetería.

   Dónde   Cuándo   Cuál   Cuánto

5. —¿ _____ estudias?—Estudio por la noche todos los días de la semana.

   Quién   Por qué   Cuándo   Cómo

6. —¿ _____ sacas buenas notas? —Porque estudio mucho.

   Dónde   Cuáles   Cómo   Por qué

7. —¿ _____ es tu profesor favorito? —Mi profesor favorito es el de historia.

   Quién   Cómo   Dónde   Cuánto

1-37   La entrevista. A reporter from the school newspaper is interviewing you about your experience at the university. Answer the reporter's questions so that he can write an article about you.

REPORTERO: Hola, ¿cómo estás?

TÚ: (1) _____

REPORTERO: ¿Cómo te llamas?

TÚ: (2) _____

REPORTERO: ¿Quién es tu profesor/a favorito/a?

TÚ: (3) _____

REPORTERO: ¿Dónde vives en el campus?

TÚ: (4) _____

REPORTERO: ¿Cuántas clases tomas este semestre?

TÚ: (5) _____

REPORTERO: ¿Qué clases tomas este semestre?

TÚ: (6) _____

REPORTERO: ¿Cómo son tus clases?

TÚ: (7) _____

REPORTERO: ¿Dónde comes normalmente (*ordinarily*)?

TÚ: (8) _____

REPORTERO: ¿Cómo son tus notas?

TÚ: (9) _____

REPORTERO: ¿Cuáles son tus materias favoritas?

TÚ: (10) _____

REPORTERO: Muchas gracias por tu tiempo.

TÚ: De nada. Hasta luego.

1-38   Otra entrevista. This time, your classmate Sara wants to find out about some of the activities you do in your free time (**tiempo libre**). Listen carefully to her six questions, and then answer them orally using the vocabulary you have learned in *Capítulo 1*.

1. ...   2. ...   3. ...   4. ...   5. ...   6. ...

MOSAICOS

A escuchar

Antes de escuchar

1-39   ¿Es típico? While studying abroad, Daniel has found that many aspects of his lifestyle and routine in the United States are not so common among his new friends in Spain. Make a list in Spanish of habits or routines that may be typical of American college students, but that might not be typical for students in other countries.

_____

_____

_____

_____

_____

Escuchar

1-40   ¿Similares? Listen once for the gist of the passage. From what you have heard, do you think you and Daniel have a lot of behaviors in common?

Listen again and select **Sí** if Daniel mentions an activity below, or **No** if he does not.

1.	Limpia el apartamento los fines de semana.	Sí	No
2.	Hace ejercicio en el gimnasio de la universidad.	Sí	No
3.	Estudia en la biblioteca.	Sí	No
4.	Come en la cafetería o en un restaurante.	Sí	No
5.	Monta en bicicleta en el campus de la universidad.	Sí	No

Después de escuchar

1-41   Más actividades. Now write the activities or routines from your list that Daniel did not mention.

_____

_____

_____

¿Tienen ustedes mucho en común (*in common*)? _____

A conversar

1-42   Más preguntas. You have learned a lot about Daniel and his study abroad experience, but you still have more questions. You call him and reach his voice mail. Leave a message for Daniel and ask at least five questions orally, so that you can gather more information about his university life in Spain.

A leer

Antes de leer

1-43   Preparación. Look at the following text and identify what type of text it is.

a. un artículo   **b.** un anuncio (*ad*)   **c.** un ensayo (*essay*)

La Universidad de Deusto, un centro jesuita de enseñanza e investigación (*teaching and research*) con larga (*long*) tradición, es una de las instituciones privadas más prestigiosas de España. Dos ex-presidentes de España y varios congresistas son ex-alumnos (*alumni*) de esta universidad. Cada año estudiantes de todo el mundo vienen a la Universidad de Deusto. La universidad está en un lugar (*place*) excelente, enfrente del Museo Guggenheim, en Bilbao, en el centro de la ciudad. Los profesores utilizan tecnología moderna en sus clases.

La universidad ofrece (*offers*) muchos cursos para extranjeros (*foreign students*):

SEMESTRE:

- Español 1, 2 y 3
- Civilización y cultura españolas
- Cultura y lengua vascas (*Basque*)
- Español para negocios (*business*)
- Cine y literatura española
- Literatura española: Siglos XVI-XVII
- Literatura española: Siglos XVIII-XIX
- Literatura española: Siglo XX
- Ficción española: Siglo XX
- Composición y sintaxis del español
- Historia de España hasta el siglo XVIII
- Variedades de español
- Europa en el mundo

VERANO (SUMMER SESSION):

- Español 1, 2 y 3
- Civilización y cultura españolas
- Literatura española: Siglo XX
- España en Europa
- Español académico

Las Facultades de Ingeniería, Economía y otras suplementan la oferta básica. Además, hay excursiones guiadas (*guided tours*) a Madrid, Segovia, Toledo, Burgos, el sur de Francia y Pamplona.

Leer

1-44   La Universidad de Deusto. Now, read each statement given below. Then read the text in its entirety, and finally indicate whether the following sentences are **Cierto** or **Falso**.

1. En la Universidad de Deusto hay pocos (*few*) cursos de español para extranjeros (*foreigners*).	Cierto	Falso
2. La Universidad de Deusto es una institución nueva (*new*).	Cierto	Falso
3. La Universidad de Deusto no usa tecnología.	Cierto	Falso
4. En la Universidad de Deusto hay clases sobre muchas disciplinas (*subjects*).	Cierto	Falso
5. En el programa para extranjeros de la Universidad de Deusto hay sólo (*only*) clases de español.	Cierto	Falso

Después de leer

1-45   ¡Deseo solicitar! After reading the announcement for the University of Deusto, you decide to study abroad for one year. Fill out the following application form with the necessary information.

Universidad de Deusto

Solicitud de Admisión

Curso académico 20 _____   20 _____

Nombre:

Dirección:

Calle y número:

Ciudad   Estado/Provincia (*State*)   País (*Country*)

¿Qué cursos desea (*do you wish*) tomar?

¿En qué universidad estudia usted ahora?

Por la presente solicito la admisión al programa para estudiantes extranjeros de la Universidad de Deusto.

   Firma   Fecha

   _____

   _____

   _____

   _____

   _____

A escribir

Antes de escribir

1-46 Preparación. You have decided to study at the Universidad de Deusto. In addition to the application form, you need to send a letter about yourself. Before you write the letter, write down in Spanish three words that describe your personality and three that indicate your interests.

_____

_____

_____

Escribir

1-47 Carta de presentación. Now, write a letter to the dean of Admissions describing yourself. Also mention your field(s) of interest, and give two reasons why you want to study in Deusto.

_____

_____

_____

_____

_____

_____

_____

_____

Después de escribir

1-48   Revisión. Go over your letter carefully, and if possible, ask a classmate or your instructor for feedback. Revisit your textbook for correct vocabulary, grammar and spelling. Finally, rewrite your letter, adding any important information that you left out.

_____

_____

_____

_____

_____

_____

_____

Firma

ENFOQUE CULTURAL

1-49 Escuelas y universidades en España. Reread the *Enfoque cultural* section in your textbook, and then select whether the following statements are **Cierto** or **Falso**.

1. Muchas de las universidades en España son muy antiguas.   Cierto   Falso

2. El sistema escolar en España es muy similar al sistema de Estados Unidos.   Cierto   Falso

3. La Universidad de Salamanca tiene un programa de español para extranjeros.   Cierto   Falso

4. En general, los estudiantes españoles no practican muchos deportes.   Cierto   Falso

5. A los estudiantes españoles les gusta escuchar música.   Cierto   Falso

6. La música típica de Sevilla es el rock español.   Cierto   Falso

7. Hay muchos bares de tapas cerca de la Ciudad Universitaria.   Cierto   Falso

1-50 Las universidades españolas. Use the search engines you find at the *Mosaicos* website to find the name of a university in each of the cities on the list.

Madrid _____

Barcelona _____

Sevilla _____

Córdoba _____

Valencia _____

Alicante _____

Castellón _____

Granada _____

Valladolid _____

Now, visit the web pages of the universities you have found. Write the name(s) of the university or universities that offer(s) courses in the following subjects.

la psicología _____

la antropología _____

la economía _____

la literatura _____

la historia _____

REPASO

1-51   El salón de clase. Emilia, one of Daniel's friends, needs to purchase some new classroom supplies to use in her classes. Help her by labeling the pictures with the correct words, and be sure to use the correct indefinite articles.

1.

_____

2.

_____

3.

_____

4.

_____

5.

_____

1-52   Los lugares. Emilia is new to the university and she wants to become acquainted with university life. Help her by matching the most appropriate activity with each of the places listed below.

_____ 1. la librería   **a.** hablar y escuchar español

_____ 2. la biblioteca   **b.** comer con los amigos

_____ 3. el café   **c.** comprar libros

_____ 4. la discoteca   **d.** bailar

_____ 5. el laboratorio de lenguas   **e.** estudiar

1-53   La primera semana de clase. It is Emilia's first semester of Spanish, and at the end of the first week she wants to show the professor what she has learned. Help her to complete the following conversation with the appropriate expressions.

Emilia: _____

Profesora Sánchez: Buenos días. Soy la Profesora Sánchez. ¿Cómo te llamas?

Emilia: _____

Profesora Sánchez: Igualmente. ¿Cómo estás hoy?

Emilia: _____

Profesora Sánchez: Bien, gracias. Bueno, tengo otra clase en diez minutos. Hasta mañana.

Emilia: _____

1-54 Preguntas y más preguntas. Emilia has just met Juan Carlos, a student in her Spanish class. In order to find out more about him, she asks him questions about his academic and personal life. Use the interrogative words you have learned to complete their conversation.

EMILIA: Hola, Juan Carlos. ¿Cómo estás?

JUAN CARLOS: Hola, ¿qué tal?

EMILIA: Bien. (1) _____

JUAN CARLOS: Yo estudio español, economía y matemáticas. ¿Y tú?

EMILIA: ¡Qué bien! Yo también estudio español.

(2) _____

JUAN CARLOS: Mi clase favorita es español.

EMILIA: Ah, muy bien. ¿Y tienes muchos amigos?

JUAN CARLOS: Sí, muchos.

EMILIA: (3) _____

JUAN CARLOS: Se llaman Julio, Patricia y Pilar.

EMILIA: En mi clase hay nueve estudiantes.

(4) _____

JUAN CARLOS: En mi clase hay diez estudiantes.

EMILIA: Excelente. Después de la universidad yo trabajo en un restaurante.

(5) _____

JUAN CARLOS: Yo trabajo en la biblioteca.

EMILIA: ¡Ah, qué bien! Bueno, nos vemos pronto, Juan Carlos. Chao.

JUAN CARLOS: Hasta pronto.

1-55 Mi primer día de clases. Listen to the conversation between two of Emilia's classmates, and then indicate whether the following statements are **Cierto** or **Falso**.

1. Iris está en la clase de la Sra. Kelly.	Cierto	Falso
2. El esposo de la Sra. Kelly es de Buenos Aires.	Cierto	Falso
3. La clase de la Sra. Kelly no es muy interesante.	Cierto	Falso
4. Los estudiantes en la clase de la Sra. Kelly miran la televisión.	Cierto	Falso
5. En la clase de español hay tarea de lunes a viernes.	Cierto	Falso

1-56   La Universidad de Granada. Emilia would like to know more about the universities in Spain. Help her by reading this article you researched, and then indicate whether the sentences that follow are **Cierto** or **Falso**.

El sistema universitario español y el norteamericano tienen características comunes. En la Universidad de Granada, por ejemplo, los estudiantes tienen la posibilidad de tomar los mismos (*the same*) cursos que en Estados Unidos. Hay facultades de arquitectura, ciencias, humanidades y medicina, entre otras, en la Universidad de Granada. Además, los estudiantes con muy buenas notas tienen la oportunidad de solicitar becas (*scholarships*), aunque (*although*) la mayoría de las becas son para las ciencias y la medicina.

Sin embargo (*however*), hay diferencias entre los dos sistemas también. Las clases en Granada empiezan (*begin*) entre el 1 y el 7 de octubre y terminan en junio. Además, la universidad ofrece beneficios para las familias con muchos hijos (*children*). Para las familias numerosas, no es necesario pagar por la educación universitaria. Ésta es probablemente la diferencia más grande entre la Universidad de Granada y las universidades norteamericanas.

1.	Los sistemas universitarios en España y en Estados Unidos tienen algunas características comunes.	Cierto	Falso
2.	Muchas de las becas son para las humanidades.	Cierto	Falso
3.	La Universidad de Granada ofrece clases para niños.	Cierto	Falso
4.	Las clases en la Universidad de Granada empiezan en octubre.	Cierto	Falso
5.	La diferencia más grande entre los dos sistemas es el tipo de cursos que ofrecen.	Cierto	Falso

Nombre: _____

Fecha: _____

Mis amigos y yo

A PRIMERA VISTA

2-1 ¿Quién es? Look at the illustrations of the four people below and think about some of the words and expressions you might use to describe each person. Now listen to each description and match it with the corresponding drawing.

1. _____   2. _____   3. _____   4. _____

2-2 ¿Es cierto? Read the following sentences about the characteristics of several famous people and indicate whether they are true (**Cierto**) or false (**Falso**). If you are unsure of who these people are, try looking them up on your favorite search engine.

1. Danny De Vito es bajo.	Cierto	Falso
2. Bill Gates es rico.	Cierto	Falso
3. Jennifer López es soltera.	Cierto	Falso
4. Eva Longoria es delgada.	Cierto	Falso
5. Chris Rock es moreno.	Cierto	Falso
6. Katie Holmes es joven.	Cierto	Falso
7. Ricky Martin es bilingüe.	Cierto	Falso
8. Salma Hayek es rubia.	Cierto	Falso

2-3   Completamente diferentes. Your friends Susana and Marta do not look anything alike. In fact, Marta is the exact opposite of Susana. Based on the words given to describe Susana, write the opposite word to describe Marta.

SUSANA	MARTA
1. alta	_____
2. gorda	_____
3. rubia	_____
4. extrovertida	_____
5. fuerte	_____
6. trabajadora	_____
7. simpática	_____

2-4   ¿Cómo son? Now, write a descriptive word for each of the following people. For more information about the celebrities, you may look them up on your favorite search engine.

1. Lebron James   _____
2. Penélope Cruz   _____
3. Oprah Winfrey   _____
4. Arnold Schwarzenegger   _____
5. Robert DeNiro   _____
6. el profesor/la profesora de español   _____
7. su compañero/a de cuarto   _____

2-5   La nueva amiga de Rafael. Some of the rumors you have heard about Rafael's new friend are inaccurate. Read the statements below. Then listen to the conversation between two of Rafael's friends and indicate whether the information is true (**Cierto**) or false (**Falso**).

1. La amiga de Rafael se llama Antonia.	Cierto	Falso
2. Antonia es norteamericana.	Cierto	Falso
3. Estudia en la universidad este semestre.	Cierto	Falso
4. Tiene dieciocho años.	Cierto	Falso
5. Desea ser profesora de economía.	Cierto	Falso

2-6 Más amigos hispanos. You have just met some native Spanish-speaking students, Ernesto, Ana, Claudia, and David, at the Hispanic Cultural Center at your university. Listen to them describe themselves, and then write the name of the person that best answers each question.

1. ¿Quién tiene veintidós años y es morena y divertida? _____

2. ¿Quién tiene pelo negro y es alto y activo? _____

3. ¿Quién es chilena y pelirroja y tiene veintidós años? _____

4. ¿Quién es argentino, moreno y alto? _____

2-7 ¿Qué les gusta? You, Claudia and David are talking about the things you like and do not like to do. Listen to Claudia and David discuss their preferences and indicate which of them likes each activity below by selecting **Claudia, David,** or **los dos** (*both*).

1. montar en bicicleta		Claudia	David	los dos
2. practicar béisbol		Claudia	David	los dos
3. conversar con amigos en la computadora		Claudia	David	los dos
4. ir a un café		Claudia	David	los dos
5. estudiar en la biblioteca		Claudia	David	los dos

2-8 Los colores. Select the color most commonly associated with each object.

1. una banana

amarilla	verde	azul	marrón	gris

2. una esmeralda (*emerald*)

morada	blanca	gris	verde	azul

3. una pizarra

roja	negra	carmelita	anaranjada	rosada

4. la nieve (*snow*)

azul	rosa	blanca	gris	negra

5. el café

verde	marrón	amarillo	morado	gris

2-9   Nacionalidades. Can you identify the countries of origin for each of the following celebrities? Choose the correct country from the word bank and write the adjective of nationality. If you are unsure about where each person comes from, try looking them up on your favorite search engine.

Colombia	España	Guatemala	Puerto Rico
Cuba	Estados Unidos	México	Venezuela

1. Ricky Martin es _____.

2. Carolina Herrera es _____.

3. Fidel Castro es _____.

4. Enrique Iglesias es _____.

5. Jennifer López es _____.

6. Rigoberta Menchú es _____.

7. Emiliano Zapata es _____.

8. Gabriel García Márquez es _____.

2-10   Crucigrama. Read the following clues and complete the crossword puzzle with the correct vocabulary words.

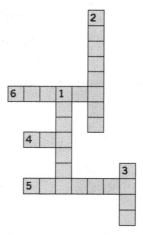

VERTICALES

1. La nacionalidad de Antonio Banderas

2. La nacionalidad de Salma Hayek

3. Uno de los colores de la bandera de Estados Unidos

HORIZONTALES

4. Una muchacha que no es bonita es…

5. No es gordo; es…

6. Una chica con pelo negro es…

EN ACCIÓN

2-11   Antes de ver. Do you remember what the main characters in the video are like? Indicate whether the following statements refer to Javier (**J**), Daniel (**D**), Gabi (**G**), or Luciana (**L**).

1. La chivita es su mejor amiga. _____

2. Es la amiga de Gabi. _____

3. Es simpático y cómico. _____

4. Tiene un teléfono celular nuevo. _____

5. Es muy puntual. _____

2-12   Mientras ve. As you watch the segment, complete following description of Beatriz Condes.

bonita	castaño	largo	negros	nerviosa	veinte

Beatriz es (1) _____. Tiene el pelo (2) _____ y (3) _____. Tiene los ojos (4) _____. Tiene (5) _____ años. Está un poco (6) _____, pero está lista para cantar.

2-13   Después de ver. Daniel seems to be very interested in Beatriz's audition. Now that you have seen the episode, write a brief description of Daniel's reaction to her.

_____

_____

_____

_____

_____

_____

FUNCIONES Y FORMAS

1. Describing people, places, and things: Adjectives (Textbook p. 64)

2-14   ¿Quién es? Listen to the following adjectives, decide whether each describes **Ana, Ernesto, Ernesto y David,** or **Ana o Ernesto,** and select the correct name(s). Remember that Spanish adjectives agree in gender and number with the nouns they describe.

1. Ana   Ernesto   Ernesto y David   Ana o Ernesto
2. Ana   Ernesto   Ernesto y David   Ana o Ernesto
3. Ana   Ernesto   Ernesto y David   Ana o Ernesto
4. Ana   Ernesto   Ernesto y David   Ana o Ernesto
5. Ana   Ernesto   Ernesto y David   Ana o Ernesto
6. Ana   Ernesto   Ernesto y David   Ana o Ernesto
7. Ana   Ernesto   Ernesto y David   Ana o Ernesto
8. Ana   Ernesto   Ernesto y David   Ana o Ernesto

2-15   La universidad. The following adjectives describe objects and people you can find on a university campus. Read each adjective and indicate the object or person being described.

1. aburridas
   las profesoras   la historia   los libros   la estudiante

2. sincero
   mis amigas   el rector   la actriz   mis profesores

3. necesarios
   el diccionario   las clases   la biblioteca   los cuadernos

4. optimista
   el estudiante   las chicas   los amigos   las profesoras

5. moderno
   el laboratorio   los libros   las clases   la biblioteca

2-16   ¿Cómo son? Your friend Rafael knows some other Hispanic students, and he wants you to meet them. First read what Rafael says. Then listen to him and fill in the missing adjectives.

Sí, Nico y Elsa son (1) _____. Son muy (2) _____, y me gusta mucho conversar con ellos. Nico es muy (3) _____ y (4) _____. Elsa es más (5) _____, pero es (6) _____ también. Elsa estudia economía y es muy (7) _____ y (8) _____. Todos los días estudia mucho en la biblioteca. Nico también es (9) _____, aunque es un poco (10) _____.

2-17   Cualidades esenciales. You and a friend are discussing the qualities that you think a good friend must have. Write a list of these qualities in complete sentences below.

MODELO: *Un buen amigo es...*

1. _____

2. _____

3. _____

4. _____

5. _____

6. _____

2-18   ¿Cómo es usted? You are very excited because you are going to Mexico on a study-abroad program. Write an e-mail message to your host family to introduce yourself, and include a description of your physical characteristics and personality traits.

De: _____

A: _____

Tema: ¡Hola! Soy yo...

_____

_____

_____

_____

2. Identifying and describing: expressing origin, possession, location of events, and time: Present tense of *ser* (Textbook p. 67)

2-19   El concierto de Marc Anthony. The local radio announcers are talking about Marc Anthony, who is in town for a concert. Read the following statements; then listen to the information and indicate if each sentence below is true (**Cierto**) or false (**Falso**).

1. Marc Anthony es puertorriqueño.   Cierto   Falso

2. Marc Anthony es de Nueva York.   Cierto   Falso

3. Sus padres (*parents*) son de Puerto Rico.   Cierto   Falso

4. Es bilingüe: habla inglés y francés.   Cierto   Falso

5. Marc Anthony es muy divertido.   Cierto   Falso

6. Su concierto es esta noche, en la plaza.   Cierto   Falso

2-20   Las personas en la universidad. Rafael is describing some of the people in his university. Complete the sentences with the correct form of **ser**.

1. Mi profesora favorita _____ fantástica.

2. Mis compañeros _____ simpáticos y alegres.

3. Yo _____ un estudiante inteligente.

4. Mi mejor amigo _____ muy trabajador.

5. Nosotros _____ jóvenes y alegres.

6. Tú _____ soltero/a.

2-21   ¿Cómo son? Think about your life at the university and the things you have there, and describe the following people, places or things. Be sure to modify the adjectives as necessary so that they agree with the things or people being described.

MODELO: La profesora de español *es inteligente y simpática.*

1. Mi compañero/a de cuarto _____

2. Mi mejor amigo en la universidad _____

3. Mis clases _____

4. La cafetería _____

5. Yo _____

2-22   ¿De quién es? Think about the people in your Spanish class, and answer the following questions with complete sentences to indicate a logical owner for each object.

MODELO: ¿De quién es la calculadora?

   Es de Julieta.

1. ¿De quién es el bolígrafo?

   _____

2. ¿De quién son los libros?

   _____

3. ¿De quién es la computadora?

   _____

4. ¿De quién son los discos compactos?

   _____

5. ¿De quién es el cuaderno?

   _____

6. ¿De quién es la mochila?

   _____

2-23   Hora y lugar. Tomorrow is Saturday. You already know about the Marc Anthony concert, but Rafael wants to tell you about the other activities going on. Listen to Rafael and complete each sentence with the correct information.

1. El concierto de Marc Anthony es a las _____ de la _____.
2. La conferencia sobre el Amazonas es en _____.
3. El baile de la Asociación de Estudiantes es en _____.
4. La película *Diarios de motocicleta* es a las _____.

3. Expressing inherent qualities and changeable conditions: *Ser* and *estar* with adjectives (Textbook p. 70)

2-24   Una conversación telefónica. Rafael's mother is away from home on a business trip, and she has just called to find out how things are going at home. Complete the conversation by writing the correct forms of **ser** or **estar**.

RAFAEL: Hola mamá! ¿Cómo (1) _____ tú?

MAMÁ: Estoy bien, ¿y tú?

RAFAEL: Bien. ¿Dónde estás?

MAMÁ: (2) _____ en mi habitación del hotel.

RAFAEL: ¿Cómo se llama el hotel?

MAMÁ: Es el Hotel Victoria.

RAFAEL: ¿Cómo es?

MAMÁ: (3) _____ grande y lujoso.

RAFAEL: ¿(4) _____ enfrente de la playa?

MAMÁ: No, no hay playa cerca. ¿Dónde (5) _____ tu padre?

RAFAEL: Papá (6) _____ en el supermercado.

MAMÁ: Bueno, (7) _____ tarde, y tengo una reunión ahora. ¡Hasta pronto!

2-25 ¿Qué pasa? Read the following statements about Ana and decide how she is and/or feels in these situations. Be sure to write the appropriate form of the verbs **ser** or **estar** and the correct adjective from the word bank.

aburrido/a	gordo/a	trabajador/a
cansado/a	inteligente	triste

MODELO: A Ana le gusta hablar con sus amigos. *Es conversadora.*

1. Ana practica gimnasia rítmica por (*for*) dos horas. _____

2. Ana come muchos chocolates y dulces últimamente (*lately*). _____

3. Ana está en casa y no hace nada (*nothing*). _____

4. Ana trabaja todos los días. _____

5. Ana es una estudiante excelente y saca muy buenas notas. _____

6. Ana asiste a un funeral. _____

2-26 Mi vida en la universidad. Ana tells you more about her life at the university in Santo Domingo where she is spending a few weeks. Fill in the missing forms of **ser** or **estar** to complete Ana's description.

La vida (*Life*) en Santo Domingo (1) _____ muy interesante. La universidad (2) _____ grande y antigua, y mis clases (3) _____ buenas. Hoy yo (4) _____ un poco nerviosa porque tengo un examen en mi clase de literatura. La clase (5) _____ interesante, pero el profesor (6) _____ muy exigente. Tengo muchos amigos y estudio con un grupo de compañeros. Nosotros (7) _____ seis estudiantes en la clase, y estudiamos juntos (*together*) los martes por la noche. Mis amigos (8) _____ nerviosos también por (*on account of*) el examen. Yo (9) _____ muy cansada, pero (10) _____ contenta aquí porque Santo Domingo y la universidad son espectaculares.

2-27 Diferentes. Everybody seems to be acting differently these days! Listen to Rafael's statements and express how the following people are behaving. Be sure to use the correct form of **estar** and an appropriate adjective.

MODELO: You hear: Claudia es agradable.

You write: Sí, pero ahora *está enojada.*

1. Sí, pero ahora _____.

2. Sí, pero ahora _____.

3. Sí, pero ahora _____.

4. Sí, pero ahora _____.

2-28   Una entrevista. You work for the school newspaper, and you are writing an article about the students' reactions to final exams. You have decided to interview your roommate. Complete the questions you are going to ask him/her by writing the correct form of **ser** or **estar**.

1. ¿ _____ contento/a en la universidad?

2. ¿ _____ inteligentes tus profesores?

3. ¿ _____ nervioso/a por tus exámenes?

4. ¿ _____ difíciles tus exámenes?

5. ¿ _____ listo/a para los exámenes?

6. ¿ _____ un/a estudiante responsable y trabajador/a?

2-29   Ahora usted. Your roommate would like to know your answers to the interview questions in **2-28**. Answer the questions orally in complete sentences, remembering to start each one with the correct form of **ser** or **estar.**

1. ¿ _____ contento/a en la universidad?

2. ¿ _____ inteligentes tus profesores?

3. ¿ _____ nervioso/a por tus exámenes?

4. ¿ _____ difíciles tus exámenes?

5. ¿ _____ listo/a para los exámenes?

6. ¿ _____ un/a estudiante responsable y trabajador/a?

4. Expressing ownership: Possessive adjectives (Textbook p. 73)

2-30   El examen de español. The Spanish professor is speaking to her class about their upcoming exam. Complete the conversation by filling in the appropriate possessive adjectives.

PROFESORA: Bien, clase. Entonces, el examen es lunes. No olviden (1) _____ bolígrafos y (2) _____ cuadernos.

RAFAEL: Profesora, ¿puedo usar (3) _____ diccionario durante el examen?

PROFESORA: No, Rafael, no está bien usar (4) _____ diccionario durante el examen.

MARÍA: Profesora, ¿podemos usar (5) _____ libros en el examen?

PROFESORA: No, María. No deben usar (6) _____ libros. Todos los estudiantes necesitan hacer (7) _____ tarea antes del examen.

2-31 ¡A la playa! Some of your friends at school are going to spend Saturday morning at the beach, and you want your friend Roberto to come along. Fill in the blanks with the correct form of the appropriate possessive adjective.

USTED: Mañana vienes (*you are coming*) a la playa con nosotros, ¿verdad?

ROBERTO: No, (1) _____ examen de matemáticas es el lunes, y quiero estudiar.

USTED: Pero si (2) _____ examen es el lunes, estudias el domingo.

ROBERTO: Quiero estudiar todo el fin de semana. El profesor García es muy exigente (*demanding*), y (3) _____ exámenes son siempre muy difíciles.

USTED: Es más (*more*) divertido estar en la playa… además viene (4) _____ amiga favorita…

ROBERTO: ¿Susana?

USTED: Sí, todos (5) _____ amigos vienen.

ROBERTO: Muy bien, entonces estudio el domingo. Pero no quiero sacar una mala nota en (6) _____ examen.

2-32 Cosas y personas favoritas. Do you know your best friend well? Think of the things he/she likes, and complete each sentence about his/her favorite things.

MODELO: Su color favorito es *morado*.

1. _____ programa de televisión favorito es _____.

2. _____ actor/actriz favorito/a es _____.

3. _____ restaurante favorito es _____.

4. _____ grupos musicales favoritos son _____.

5. _____ clases favoritas son _____.

6. _____ actividades favoritas son _____.

2-33 ¿Qué opinas? Give your opinion about the following people or things. Be sure to use the possessive adjective and the word that best describes how you feel about each one.

MODELO: su hermano: *Mi hermano es divertido.*

1. la música de Kanye West: _____

2. los padres (*parents*) de su amigo: _____

3. sus exámenes: _____

4. sus vacaciones: _____

5. su madre: _____

6. la novia de su amigo: _____

2-34   Los planes del verano. You are reading an article in the school newspaper about the summer plans of some students. Complete the article by filling in the appropriate possessive adjectives.

¡Llegan las vacaciones de verano! Muchos estudiantes visitan a (1) _____ familias, o viajan (*travel*) con (2) _____ amigos. Por ejemplo, Diego y Alfredo son dos hermanos (*brothers*) que viven en Miami con (3) _____ padres (*parents*). (4) _____ abuelos (*grandparents*) viven en Argentina. Este verano, Diego y Alfredo visitan a (5) _____ abuelos en Buenos Aires. (6) _____ amigo Julio y yo viajamos a California para visitar a (7) _____ amiga Ana, que estudia en Los Ángeles. Carlos y Diana no viajan porque trabajan este verano. Carlos trabaja en una oficina; (8) _____ trabajo es muy fácil. Diana trabaja en un laboratorio; (9) _____ experimentos son muy interesantes.

5. Expressing likes and dislikes: *Gustar* (Textbook p. 76)

2-35   ¿Qué les gusta? Indicate what the following people like or dislike, based on the form of **gustar** that is used.

1. A mí no me gusta…
   a. las clases por la tarde.
   b. la clase de alemán.
   c. los conciertos de jazz.
   d. las ciencias sociales.

2. A los norteamericanos les gusta…
   a. las clases interesantes.
   b. los fines de semana.
   c. mirar televisión.
   d. las vacaciones.

3. A los estudiantes no les gusta…
   a. las ciencias.
   b. estudiar mucho.
   c. los exámenes.
   d. las matemáticas.

4. A mi amigo le gustan…
   a. las fiestas.
   b. bailar tango.
   c. usar la computadora.
   d. la música clásica.

5. A mi hermana (*sister*) le gusta…
   a. los videojuegos.
   b. leer en la biblioteca.
   c. las películas (*films*) cómicas.
   d. los libros de ciencia ficción.

6. A mi mejor amiga y a mí nos gustan…
   a. la universidad.
   b. tomar café.
   c. el chocolate.
   d. los coches nuevos.

2-36   ¿Te gusta? Write sentences to express your likes and dislikes about the following topics. Be sure to use the correct form of **gustar** and follow the model exactly.

MODELO: los gimnasios: *Me gustan los gimnasios.* o

No me gustan los gimnasios.

1. las discotecas: _____

2. la arquitectura colonial: _____

3. las películas de Brad Pitt: _____

4. estudiar: _____

5. cantar: _____

2-37   ¿Les gusta? Now think about your family and friends. Complete the sentences to indicate how the following people feel about each of these things. Be sure to use the correct form of **gustar**.

MODELO: A mi primo *le gusta* (o) *no le gusta* el teatro.

1. A mi madre _____ los libros de John Grisham.

2. A mi hermano/a _____ la música de Eminem.

3. A mi mejor amigo/a _____ las comedias.

4. A mis amigos _____ bailar en las fiestas.

5. A mi padre _____ viajar.

2-38   Un nuevo compañero de cuarto. You are looking for a new roommate with whom you will be compatible, so you decide to put an ad on Craigslist. First, give a description of yourself orally. Specifically mention the things you like and dislike, and then describe the kind of roommate you are looking for.

MOSAICOS

A escuchar

Antes de escuchar

2-39   Preparación. You will hear two friends talk about Miguel Hernández, a nineteen-year-old exchange student. Before you listen, list two expressions in each of the following categories that may be used to describe him.

características físicas: _____

personalidad: _____

Escuchar

2-40   Un estudiante de intercambio. Now listen to the conversation and focus on the specific information you need to answer the following questions. Be sure to give only one-word answers.

1. ¿De qué nacionalidad es Miguel Hernández? _____

2. ¿Cómo es su pelo? _____

3. ¿Qué clase tiene Miguel? _____

4. ¿Cuántos años tiene? _____

5. ¿Es simpático o antipático? _____

6. ¿Es inteligente o tonto? _____

Después de escuchar

2-41   ¿Qué tienen en común? Do you and Miguel have anything in common? List two or three similarities or differences.

_____

_____

_____

A conversar

2-42   Su media naranja (*other half*). You are thinking about trying an online dating service, and you must record a detailed description of yourself for other prospective daters. Be sure to include a description of your physical and personality traits, as well as your likes and dislikes. Also, mention how you feel about joining the dating service.

A leer

Antes de leer

2-43   ¿Qué tipo de texto es? Read the title of the following text and look at the format. What type of text is it?

_____

Leer

2-44   Citas por Internet. Read the following statements below. Then read the ad about online dating, and indicate whether each statement is true (**Cierto**) or false (**Falso**) according to the information given.

Amor Verdadero: Servicio de citas por Internet

¡Enamórate (fall in love) *por las razones correctas!*

Hay más de 100 millones de solteros en el mundo. ¡Buenas noticias!, ¿verdad? Pero a veces encontrar una pareja (*partner*) es muy difícil, especialmente la persona correcta.

Este servicio de Internet es para solteros que buscan relaciones REALES. Los anuncios personales describen con mucho detalle (*detail*) las características físicas y de personalidad de los miembros (*members*).

Hay más de 3 millones de miembros de Amor Verdadero, y más de 50.000 personas se convierten en miembros cada semana. Hay muchos videos y miles (*thousands*) de grabaciones disponibles (*recordings available*) en nuestra página web. También hay servicios de mensajes instantáneos con video, audio y texto, y líneas de chat.

Ponga su anuncio GRATIS para encontrar a su pareja ideal.

---

1. Amor Verdadero tiene muchos miembros activos.	Cierto	Falso
2. En Amor Verdadero usted usa el teléfono para comunicarse con otros miembros.	Cierto	Falso
3. Amor Verdadero es un servicio para buscar pareja.	Cierto	Falso
4. Poner su anuncio cuesta mucho dinero.	Cierto	Falso
5. Amor Verdadero usa mucha tecnología.	Cierto	Falso

Después de leer

2-45   Su perfil. After reading the ad for *Amor Verdadero*, you have decided to submit your profile. Fill in the following profile with appropriate real or imagined personal information.

Amor Verdadero

¡Enamórate por las razones correctas!

Nombre: Sexo: Hombre   Mujer

Dirección: Edad:

Número de teléfono: Nacionalidad:

Dirección de correo electrónico (*e-mail*):

Características físicas:

Características de personalidad:

Gustos (aficiones [*hobbies*], intereses, actividades favoritas):

¿Qué tipo de persona busca usted? (edad [*age*], características físicas y de personalidad)

¿Por qué desea usar Amor Verdadero?

_____

_____

_____

_____

_____

_____

_____

_____

_____

_____

_____

_____

_____

_____

A escribir

Antes de escribir

2-46   ¡Por fin! You have received a response from *Amor Verdadero* with the profile of two people you might be interested in. Read the statements that follow and look at the descriptions of each person. Then, in the numbered items, indicate who is being described by selecting **A** (for Anthony or Allyson) or **C** (for Carlos or Cristina).

If you are looking for a male companion:

Anthony **(A):**	*Carlos* **(C):**
21 años	22 años
estadounidense	argentino
estudiante	estudiante
guapo	guapo
delgado	bajo
simpático	optimista
alegre	callado
pobre	rico
trabajador	listo

If you are looking for a female companion:

Allyson **(A):**	*Cristina* **(C):**
21 años	22 años
estadounidense	argentina
estudiante	estudiante
guapa	guapa
delgada	baja
simpática	optimista
alegre	callada
pobre	rica
trabajadora	lista

1. A   C   Su actitud es siempre positiva.
2. A   C   A veces necesita dinero.
3. A   C   Habla poco (*not much*).
4. A   C   No es muy alto/a.

5. A   C   Es inteligente.
6. A   C   No es antipático/a.
7. A   C   No es gordo/a.

Escribir

2-47   La carta. Now select a person from the previous activity and write a letter to him/her. Introduce and describe yourself. Then suggest a meeting in person, and tell him/her your plans for that meeting (what you are going to do, where you are planning to go).

Querido/a _____,

_____

_____

_____

_____

_____

_____

_____

_____

_____

_____

Después de escribir

2-48   Un/a amigo/a curioso/a. You are on a date with the person you met through *Amor Verdadero*, and your best friend wants to know everything. Since your date has stepped out for a second, answer your friend's questions in complete sentences.

1. ¿Dónde están ustedes?

   _____

2. ¿Cómo están?

   _____

3. ¿Cómo es la persona?

   _____

4. ¿Cómo son sus amigos y su familia?

   _____

5. ¿Qué le gusta o no le gusta hacer (*do*)?

   _____

6. ¿Son compatibles ustedes? ¿Por qué?

   _____

ENFOQUE CULTURAL

2-49   La expansión de Estados Unidos. Read the statements below. Then reread the *Enfoque cultural* section on pages 84–85 in your textbook and finally indicate if the statements are true (**Cierto**) or false (**Falso**).

1. La primera expansión de Estados Unidos es en 1802.   Cierto   Falso

2. La compra de Luisiana está representada en la
   moneda de 25 centavos.   Cierto   Falso

3. En 1801 James Madison anexa la península de Florida.   Cierto   Falso

4. Muchos habitantes de California y Arizona son
   descendientes de mexicanos.   Cierto   Falso

5. Los habitantes de Puerto Rico no son ciudadanos
   de Estados Unidos.   Cierto   Falso

2-50   Las nacionalidades. Visit the *Mosaicos* webpage to find the nationalities of each of the following people, and write the correct adjective next to the corresponding name.

1. Pablo Neruda   _____

2. Fidel Castro   _____

3. Albert Pujols   _____

4. Rigoberta Menchú   _____

5. Ricky Martin   _____

6. Ruben Darío   _____

7. Salma Hayek   _____

8. Shakira   _____

9. Emanuel Ginóbili   _____

10. Antonio Banderas   _____

2-51   La influencia hispana en Estados Unidos. Now research and make a list of the names of five people of Hispanic origin who have made an impact in government, business, sports, art, or in the fashion world of the United States.

_____

_____

_____

_____

_____

REPASO

2-52 **¿Cómo son?** Complete the descriptions of the following people with the correct adjectives from *Capítulo 2*.

1. Él es _____.   **2.** Ella es _____.   **3.** Ella es _____.

4. Ellos son _____.   **5.** Él es _____.

2-53 **Opuestos.** Complete the following statements with the correct adjectives from *Capítulo 2*.

1. Irene no es gorda, es _____.

2. Ricardo no es tonto, es _____.

3. Jorge no es trabajador, es _____.

4. Isabel no es fea, es _____.

5. Ricardo no es antipático, es _____.

2-54   Anuncio personal. You have noticed that your friend Rafael is making a lot of friends in a chat room and you would like to meet some new people also. Write a personal ad and include the following information:

- A physical description of yourself
- Two activities you like to do and two you don't like to do
- What you do in your free time
- A description of your ideal friend

ANUNCIO PERSONAL

_____

_____

_____

_____

_____

_____

_____

_____

_____

_____

_____

_____

2-55   El auto de Rafael. Read the following sentences and then listen to the conversation between Roberto and Susana. Finally, indicate if the sentences are *Cierto* or *Falso*.

1. Hay un auto enfrente de la cafetería.	Cierto	Falso
2. El auto de Rafael está al lado de la Facultad de Ciencias.	Cierto	Falso
3. El auto de Rafael es verde.	Cierto	Falso
4. El auto azul es del profesor de arte.	Cierto	Falso
5. El auto de Rafael es un Jaguar.	Cierto	Falso

2-56   Amigos nuevos. Rafael spends a lot of time in chat rooms on the Internet, and today he is chatting under the name "Rafe." He talks with a few people, and they all ask questions to find out more about each other. Read the statements below. Then read the chat screen and finally indicate if the sentences are *Cierto* or *Falso*.

	Personas en chat
RAFE: Hola, Flamenco. ¿Cómo estás hoy?	méxicolindo
Flamenco: Bastante bien. ¿Y tú?	santiago2
RAFE: Estoy aburrido. Necesito estudiar, pero me gusta más hablar con mis amigos.	RAFE Flamenco
Flamenco: ¿Qué estudias?	guadalupe
RAFE: Estudio sociología.	chico_informática
Flamenco: Aparte de ser muy trabajador, ¿cómo eres?	
RAFE: Bueno, no soy trabajador—por eso estoy aquí en la computadora. Soy bastante perezoso a veces. No estudio mucho, sólo dos o tres horas al día. Físicamente, no soy muy alto ni muy bajo. Tengo pelo castaño y ojos color café, y uso lentes. ¿Y tú? ¿Cómo eres? ¿Qué te gusta hacer?	
Flamenco: Yo también uso lentes. Soy muy delgado porque monto en bicicleta todos los días. Tengo 26 años. No soy estudiante, pero trabajo seis días a la semana. Bueno, ahora mismo necesito trabajar. Hablamos mañana, ¿no?	
RAFE: Perfecto. Hasta luego.	
Flamenco: Adiós.	

1. Rafael está aburrido hoy.   Cierto   Falso

2. Rafael estudia biología.   Cierto   Falso

3. Rafael estudia mucho y usa lentes.   Cierto   Falso

4. "Flamenco" trabaja mucho y monta
   en bicicleta todos los días.   Cierto   Falso

5. Los chicos necesitan terminar la
   conversación porque Rafael necesita
   estudiar.   Cierto   Falso

6. Rafael es alto y tiene el pelo castaño.   Cierto   Falso

Nombre: _____

Fecha: _____

El tiempo libre

A PRIMERA VISTA

3-1   Diversiones. Listen to Daniel and Teresa describe themselves and their activities once, and focus on getting the general idea. Then listen again and indicate whether the following statements are true (**Cierto**) or false (**Falso**).

1.	Daniel va al cine con sus amigos.	Cierto	Falso
2.	Daniel escucha música en casa.	Cierto	Falso
3.	Daniel conversa con sus amigos en un café.	Cierto	Falso
4.	A Daniel le gusta hablar de política.	Cierto	Falso
5.	A Daniel no le gusta leer novelas.	Cierto	Falso
6.	Daniel nunca lee el periódico.	Cierto	Falso
7.	Teresa estudia sólo (*only*) arte.	Cierto	Falso
8.	Teresa es norteamericana.	Cierto	Falso
9.	Teresa va a Perú durante las vacaciones.	Cierto	Falso
10.	A Teresa no le gusta tocar la guitarra.	Cierto	Falso
11.	Teresa canta canciones peruanas.	Cierto	Falso
12.	A Teresa le gusta bailar en casa de sus amigos.	Cierto	Falso

3-2   ¿Dónde? Read the list of Teresa's leisure activities and indicate the most logical location for them to take place.

1. _____ ver películas
2. _____ descansar
3. _____ estudiar
4. _____ tomar el sol y nadar
5. _____ bailar y conversar

a. la biblioteca
b. el apartamento
c. una fiesta
d. el mar
e. el cine

3-3   Las rutinas. Teresa's weekly activities are grouped below. Indicate the activity in each group that does not belong.

1. **a.** bailar   **b.** ir al cine   **c.** estudiar   **d.** alquilar películas

2. **a.** cenar   **b.** desayunar   **c.** hablar   **d.** almorzar

3. **a.** montar en bicicleta   **b.** correr   **c.** practicar el fútbol **d.** descansar

4. **a.** trabajar   **b.** cantar canciones   **c.** tocar la guitarra   **d.** escuchar música

3-4   El fin de semana. You will hear three college students talk about their weekend activities. Below are the activities they will mention; write them in the order that you hear them. Mario's first activity is filled in as a model.

bailar en la discoteca	ir al cine	tomar algo en un café
conversar en la computadora	leer el periódico	tocar la guitarra
escuchar música	leer revistas	ver televisión

1. Las actividades de Mario: *leer el periódico*, _____ y _____

   _____.

2. Las actividades de Patricia:

   _____, _____ y _____.

3. Las actividades de Emilio: _____, _____ y _____

   _____.

3-5   El tiempo libre. What is your weekend usually like? Write complete sentences describing the leisure activities you usually enjoy on the weekends.

MODELO: viernes por la noche

   El viernes por la noche yo ceno en un restaurante.

1. viernes por la noche

   _____

2. sábado por la mañana

   _____

3. sábado por la noche

   _____

4. domingo por la tarde

   _____

3-6 **Este fin de semana.** You and your roommate usually have a lot of fun on the weekends and you want to invite a friend to join you. You are in a café having lunch with your friend. Explain to him/her orally what you and your roommate usually do, using the *nosotros* form, and then invite him/her to come along.

3-7 **En el supermercado.** It is your turn to go grocery shopping. Your shopping list is long, and you realize that you do not have enough money to buy everything, so you call your roommate to find out which things are essential. Listen to her and select all the items she wants you to buy.

jugo de naranja	agua mineral
leche	pollo
cereal	papas
pan	lechuga
huevos	tomate
arroz	fruta
refrescos	helado
cerveza	chocolate

3-8 **La comida.** You are thinking about going out to dinner and the food you might like to order. Complete the sentences with the most appropriate words from the word bank. Be sure not to repeat any answers.

cerveza	helado	refresco	vino
ensalada	pollo	té	

1. Una buena cena incluye el _____ y los vegetales.

2. El _____ es una bebida caliente que me fascina.

3. Un postre delicioso es el _____.

4. La coca-cola es un _____.

5. Me gusta tomar una copa de _____ con la cena.

6. Una _____ no tiene muchas calorías.

3-9   En el restaurante. Elena and Javier are going to have dinner at a restaurant in Lima. First, read the server's questions and then match each one with the response that you hear.

1. _____ Buenas tardes, señores.

2. _____ ¿Qué desea comer, señora?

3. _____ Muy bien, ¿y para beber?

4. _____ Y el señor, ¿qué quiere comer?

5. _____ La especialidad es el ceviche.

6. _____ ¿Y desea un plato principal (*main course*)?

7. _____ ¿Y desea beber cerveza también?

8. _____ ¿Desean ustedes algo más?

a. Una cerveza, por favor.

b. Pues un ceviche de camarones para mí.

c. No, cerveza no. Para mí, vino.

d. Yo, pescado con papas fritas.

e. Buenas tardes.

f. Sí, de plato principal quiero un bistec.

g. Sí, una ensalada de lechuga, por favor.

h. Uhm... ¿cuál es la especialidad de la casa?

3-10   La comida y las bebidas. Complete the following word search and identify the foods and beverages from the list. Be sure to look for words horizontally, vertically, diagonally or backwards.

agua	cerveza	hamburguesa	huevo	lechuga	pollo	sopa	vino
arroz	ensalada	helado	jugo	pescado	queso	tomate	

e	s	n	a	s	j	p	d	d	h	g	h	e
v	r	o	a	u	g	a	t	u	r	f	h	g
i	e	o	g	p	e	s	c	a	d	o	u	d
l	e	o	e	n	o	e	g	e	r	d	e	a
a	o	t	z	p	l	u	a	l	t	r	v	u
a	e	j	a	r	h	g	i	t	l	s	o	a
r	a	c	i	c	e	r	v	e	z	a	i	z
f	d	v	e	r	d	u	r	a	h	r	q	b
c	i	l	t	r	f	b	m	l	e	c	u	p
r	b	o	u	g	e	m	o	l	l	o	e	o
r	e	n	s	a	l	a	d	a	a	o	s	l
o	b	i	g	o	a	h	l	r	d	e	o	l
c	c	v	p	l	e	t	a	m	o	t	s	o

EN ACCIÓN

3-11   Antes de ver. In this segment, Javier is eating lunch in a Mexican restaurant. Before viewing the segment, make a list of possible foods and beverages that Javier might find on the menu.

COMIDAS   **BEBIDAS**

_____   _____

_____   _____

_____   _____

_____   _____

3-12   Mientras ve. As you view the segment, complete the following sentences.

1. El mesero recomienda pollo con _____.

2. Javier dice que le gusta la comida _____.

3. Javier quiere beber una _____.

4. Gabi no va a almorzar porque va a la casa de _____.

5. Por la noche, Javier y Daniel van al concierto de _____.

6. Javier no tiene _____ para pagar la cuenta.

7. _____ paga la cuenta.

3-13   Después de ver. Do you remember Javier and Daniel's plans? Write a short description of what they are going to do later.

_____

_____

_____

_____

_____

_____

FUNCIONES Y FORMAS

1. Talking about daily activities: Present tense of *hacer, poner, salir, traer,* and *oír* (Textbook p. 98)

3-14   Elena y su familia. Elena is an exchange student from Peru. Complete Elena's description of her family's routine, using the present tense forms of **salir, poner, oír, traer,** or **hacer.**

Por la mañana mi padre y mi hermano, Carlos, (1) _____ de casa a las siete de la mañana. Mi padre siempre (2) _____ la radio del auto y (3) _____ las noticias. Llegan a la universidad a las ocho. Mi padre va a la oficina, y mi hermano Carlos va a la biblioteca donde (4) _____ su tarea. Yo (5) _____ el despertador para las ocho de la mañana. Yo (6) _____ de la casa a las nueve de la mañana y llego a la universidad a las nueve y media. Primero voy a la clase de biología y (7) _____ los experimentos en el laboratorio. Cuando termino, voy a mis otras clases.

Por la noche, mi mamá (8) _____ música mientras prepara la cena. Mi padre llega a las seis, más o menos, y siempre (9) _____ pan fresco (*fresh*) para la cena. Mi hermano y yo (10) _____ la mesa, y todos cenamos juntos y hablamos de las actividades del día.

3-15   Mi rutina. Now that you know about Elena's daily routine, she would like to know more about yours. Talk about what you do in the morning, in the afternoon, and in the evening, and be sure to use the correct present tense form of the verbs.

3-16   ¿Qué hacemos? Elena and Teresa are telling Carlos about their usual weekend activities, but Carlos is confused because the girls are talking at the same time. Help Carlos make sense of what he is able to hear by filling in the dialogue below with the correct activities. Be sure to use the correct forms of the verbs.

| hacer ejercicio | poner flores | salir |
| oír música | poner la mesa | traer vino |

ELENA: El sábado por la mañana voy al gimnasio y (1) _____.

TERESA: !Qué bien! ¡A mí también me gusta mucho ir al gimnasio! Yo los sábados por la noche voy a un concierto y (2) _____.

ELENA: !Qué divertido! Me encantan los conciertos. Yo muchas veces los sábados por la noche me quedo (*I stay*) en casa, preparo la cena, (3) _____ y ceno con mi novio.

TERESA: Eso es muy romántico, ¿no?

ELENA: Sí, también (4) _____ para beber durante la cena y a veces (5) _____ para decorar la mesa.

TERESA: Yo los fines de semana no me quedo en casa; (6) _____ y paseo en el parque con mi perro o voy al cine o de compras (*shopping*).

ELENA: ¡Eres muy activa, Teresa! Un día debemos ir de compras juntas.

TERESA: ¡Por qué no!

3-17   Un día difícil. Carlos's mother wants her family to share some of the housework, but Carlos does not like doing chores. Listen to the conversation between Carlos and his mother and complete the sentences below with an appropriate verb form; you will need to use one of the verbs twice.

hacer   poner   salir   traer   oír

1. Carlos no contesta, pero él sí _____ a su mamá.

2. Carlos está ocupado porque _____ la tarea.

3. La madre de Carlos siempre _____ huevos y café para la familia.

4. Finalmente, Carlos _____ la mesa y _____ las tostadas.

5. Carlos _____ para la universidad a las 8:30 de la mañana.

3-18   Carlos también. Carlos's mother wants him to help out more at home, as his siblings do, but Carlos argues that he already does his share. Listen to Carlos's mother and write his response.

MODELO: You hear: Ellos ponen la mesa.

You write: *Yo pongo la mesa también.*

1. _____

2. _____

3. _____

4. _____

2. Expressing movement and plans: Present tense of *ir* and *ir a* + infinitive (Textbook p. 102)

3-19 **¿Adónde va de vacaciones?** Dani and Cristina are planning a vacation with some friends. They will be traveling separately at first, and then they will meet. Look at the map to get acquainted with the names of the cities the students will visit. Then listen to Dani and Cristina and write the name of the city where each is going.

1. Dani _____

2. Cristina _____

3. Elisa _____

4. Diego y Enrique _____

5. Todos los amigos _____

3-20 **Los planes.** Carlos and his friends are making plans for Saturday. Match each sentence below with the appropriate subject.

_____ **1.** Voy a las diez de la mañana con mi hermano.

_____ **2.** Van a las once de la mañana.

_____ **3.** Vamos al parque.

_____ **4.** Vas también.

_____ **5.** Va con Elena y Carlos en el auto.

a. Elena y Carlos

b. Tú

c. Yo

d. Teresa

e. Mi hermano y yo

3-21 ¿Adónde va? Read the following sentences about what Teresa and her friends need. Then complete the sentences by indicating where they are going to go to get what they need.

a la cafetería   a la librería   a la residencia estudiantil   al cine

a la discoteca   a la playa   a la universidad   al supermercado

MODELO: Yo necesito sacar (*take out*) un libro para mi clase de historia.

Yo *voy a la biblioteca.*

1. Teresa necesita comprar un libro para su clase de literatura inglesa.
Teresa _____.

2. Elena y Carlos necesitan pollo y verduras para la cena. Ellos _____.

3. Tú asistes a una clase a las once de la mañana. Tú _____.

4. Matt y yo deseamos beber café. Nosotros _____.

5. Tú deseas ver una película de Brad Pitt. Tú _____.

6. Ustedes están muy cansados y desean descansar. Ustedes _____.

7. Elena desea bailar y celebrar el fin de semana. Ella _____.

8. Teresa y su novio desean tomar el sol. Ellos _____.

3-22 Actividades y lugares. Listen to the following questions and respond in writing. Use the appropriate form of the verb **ir** and a place from the list below.

la biblioteca   el cine   la librería

la cafetería   la discoteca   la playa

MODELO: You hear: ¿Adónde va el profesor para cenar?

You write: *Va al restaurante.*

1. _____   4. _____
2. _____   5. _____
3. _____   6. _____

3-23 ¿Qué van a hacer? Consider where the following people are located and indicate what they are going to do.

_____ 1. En el café, Teresa…   **a.** van a leer libros.

_____ 2. En el cine, tú…   **b.** va a tomar un refresco.

_____ 3. En mi casa, yo…   **c.** vas a ver una película.

_____ 4. En la biblioteca, ellos…   **d.** voy a hacer la tarea.

_____ 5. En el concierto, Elena y yo…   **e.** vamos a escuchar música clásica.

3-24   ¿Qué van a hacer ahora? Complete the following sentences by indicating what you think these people are going to do in their respective locations.

comprar un libro   escuchar música   tomar una cerveza

descansar   tomar el sol   ver una película

MODELO: Teresa está en una tienda (*store*). *Ella va a comprar unos jeans.*

1. Carlos está en la librería. Carlos _____.

2. Tú estás en una fiesta en casa de tu amigo. Tú _____.

3. Los muchachos están en el cine. Ellos _____.

4. Yo estoy en mi habitación en casa. Yo _____.

5. Elena y Carlos están en la playa. Ellos _____.

6. Teresa y yo estamos en un concierto. Nosotros _____.

3-25   El fin de semana. Think about your plans for the weekend. Write down the activities you will do, using the verbs provided, as necessary.

bailar   escribir   estudiar   ir   mirar   ver

comer   escuchar   hablar   leer   trabajar

MODELO: Viernes

A las 8:30 de la noche, *voy a ir a la casa de una amiga.*

Sábado

A las 9:00 de la mañana, _____.

A las 12:30 de la tarde, _____.

A las 5:30 de la tarde, _____.

A las 10:00 de la noche, _____.

Domingo

A las 11:30 de la mañana, _____.

A las 2:00 de la tarde, _____.

A las 6:00 de la tarde, _____.

A las 9:00 de la noche, _____.

3-26   Mis planes. Carlos would like you to go to the beach with him over the weekend, but you already have plans. Look at the following pictures and tell Carlos orally about your plans for Friday, Saturday, and Sunday.

Viernes

Sábado

Domingo

3. Talking about quantity: Numbers 100 to 2.000.000 (Textbook p. 105)

3-27   Lotería. Elena, Teresa, and Carlos are playing **lotería**, and one of them has won. First, take note of the numbers that have been called, and then write the name of the winner. The person who completes the entire card will be the winner.

Números anunciados:

doscientos treinta	cuatrocientos sesenta y cinco	ochocientos cuarenta y nueve
setecientos doce	novecientos sesenta y cuatro	seiscientos cincuenta y cinco
dos mil quinientos dieciocho	quince mil setecientos doce	seis mil seis
cuatrocientos veintitrés	quinientos once	seiscientos sesenta y seis

ELENA

320	413	676
15.712	712	512
230	6.060	964
665	2.518	575

TERESA

230	511	2.518
666	712	964
849	655	423
15.712	465	6.006

CARLOS

774	656	2.185
220	475	323
612	6.066	501
849	51.612	655

Winner: _____

3-28   Identificación. You will hear one number from each of the following groups. To maximize your listening comprehension, read out loud all the numbers in each series before listening. Then choose the number you hear.

1.	277	287	368	167
2.	104	205	405	504
3.	213	312	203	103
4.	406	624	704	640
5.	100	101	110	1.000

3-29 ¿Adónde voy? You have taken a part-time job delivering for a local restaurant. As you leave with your first orders, you realize that the house numbers are missing! Listen and complete the addresses by writing the correct numerals.

1. Calle María de Molina _____

2. Plaza Mayor _____

3. Paseo de la Castellana _____

4. Calle Princesa _____

5. Calle de Lima _____

6. Avenida de la Ilustración _____

4. Stating what you know: *Saber* and *conocer* (Textbook p. 108)

3-30 Un trabajo nuevo. Carlos is applying for a summer job at one of the university offices. Listen to his interview with Sr. Martínez in the human resources department, and complete the statements below with the appropriate form of **saber** or **conocer**.

1. Carlos _____ usar computadoras.

2. Carlos _____ al profesor González.

3. Carlos _____ inglés y francés.

4. Carlos _____ que tiene que trabajar treinta horas por semana.

5. Carlos _____ a otras personas que trabajan allí.

3-31 ¿Y usted? Imagine that your Spanish professor needs an assistant, and you would like to apply for the job. Answer his questions truthfully in Spanish, in complete sentences.

MODELO: ¿Sabes usar la computadora?

Sí, sé usar la computadora.

1. _____

2. _____

3. _____

4. _____

5. _____

6. _____

3-32   La familia de su novio (boyfriend). Elena has a new boyfriend, and her mother wants to know how well Elena knows him. Complete Elena's mother's questions with the correct form of **saber** or **conocer**.

1. ¿ _____ tú a toda su familia?

2. ¿ _____ cocinar bien la mamá de tu novio?

3. ¿ Tu novio _____ tocar un instrumento musical?

4. ¿ _____ tú a sus amigos?

5. ¿ Tu novio _____ nadar?

6. ¿ Los padres (*parents*) de tu novio _____ hablar español?

3-33   El nuevo chico. Elena and Teresa are talking about a new student in the class. Complete their conversation with the correct form of **saber** or **conocer**.

ELENA: Teresa, ¿(1) _____ a ese chico?

TERESA: Sí, se llama Michael Stewart, y es muy amigo de Carlos. ¿Por qué?

ELENA: Es muy guapo y...

TERESA: Lo quieres (2) _____, ¿verdad?

ELENA: Sí, ¿(3) _____ qué estudia?

TERESA: (4) _____ que estudia ciencias económicas.

ELENA: ¿(5) _____ dónde vive?

TERESA: Creo que vive en la residencia estudiantil, pero no estoy segura. Mi hermano es el que (*the one who*) (6) _____ muy bien dónde vive.

ELENA: Mira, viene a sentarse (*sit*) donde estamos nosotras.

TERESA: Magnífico, así lo puedes (7) _____.

5. Expressing intention, means, movement, and duration: Some uses of *por* and *para* (Textbook p. 111)

3-34   Un viaje a Lima. Teresa and Elena made reservations for a vacation, and now their friends are asking them questions about it. Listen to the following questions and complete their answers with **por** or **para**.

1. La reserva es _____ nosotras.

2. _____ supuesto.

3. Vamos a nadar y a caminar _____ la playa.

4. Vamos a estar allí _____ cinco días.

3-35   Para viajar a Perú. To have a great vacation, you need to do some planning. Read the following text, in which some advice is given to tourists coming to Peru. Complete the paragraph with **por** or **para**.

Para viajar a otro país, usted debe prepararse. (1) _____ ejemplo, usted debe hacer reservas de avión y de hotel. Es posible hacer las reservas (2) _____ teléfono o (3) _____ Internet. (4) _____ supuesto, usted también debe tener un pasaporte (5) _____ viajar a Perú.

En los aeropuertos la seguridad es muy importante ahora, y muchas veces usted debe esperar (6) _____ una o dos horas. (7) _____ eso, es importante ir temprano (8) _____ el aeropuerto.

3-36   Conversación. Carlos and Elena are talking about Elena's plans for the evening. Read their conversation and then complete each sentence with *por* or *para*.

ELENA: Esta noche vamos a un restaurante. Mis amigas van (1) _____ el restaurante ahora.

CARLOS: ¿Y tú? ¿Cuándo vas?

ELENA: Yo voy a trabajar (2) _____ media hora más, y después voy.

CARLOS: ¿Vas a escribir el artículo (3) _____ la clase de historia ahora?

ELENA: No... esta noche no, pero (4) _____ mañana va a estar listo.

CARLOS: ¡Qué bien! (*Great!*)

ELENA: Después del restaurante vamos a la discoteca (5) _____ bailar.

CARLOS: ¿Qué discoteca?

ELENA: La de la calle Cuatro. Vamos a bailar (6) _____ unas horas.

CARLOS: ¿Y después?

ELENA: Después vamos a la casa de Amanda.

CARLOS: Bien, nos vemos entonces.

ELENA: Bueno, hasta pronto.

3-37   La carta. Carlos is reading a letter that his sister Ana sent him from Peru, where she is completing a study abroad program. Unfortunately, the dog got to the letter earlier and tore some parts of it. Complete the missing parts of the letter with **por** or **para**.

Hola Carlos:

¡(1) _____ fin tengo tiempo (2) _____ escribir! Escribo esta carta (3) _____ ti y (4) _____ papá. Estoy muy contenta en Lima. Me gusta mucho caminar (5) _____ las calles de la ciudad (6) _____ la tarde. Voy a clase todos los días. Las clases son difíciles, pero estudio (7) _____ tres horas todas las noches. Bueno, no tengo mucho tiempo ahora; la próxima semana escribo más.

Besos y abrazos,

Ana

MOSAICOS

A escuchar

Antes de escuchar

3-38 Perú. Think about a possible trip you might take to Peru, and fill in the following information based on your background knowledge and personal preferences.

1. número de días que vas a pasar en Perú: _____

2. ciudades que vas a visitar: _____, _____

3. precio del viaje (*trip*): _____

Escuchar

3-39 Las vacaciones de Elena y Teresa. Elena and Teresa are planning their vacation, and they discuss a travel package they have found. Listen to their conversation and select the answers to the following questions.

1. ¿Adónde van a ir Elena y Teresa?

  a. a Lima   **b.** a tres ciudades en Perú   **c.** a Miami

2. ¿Por cuántos días van a ir?

  a. siete días   **b.** diez días   **c.** dos semanas

3. ¿Cuánto cuestan las vacaciones?

  a. 250 dólares   **b.** 25.000 dólares   **c.** 2.500 dólares

4. ¿Dónde hay restaurantes buenos?

  a. en Cuzco   **b.** en Lima   **c.** en Machu Picchu

5. ¿Para qué van a llamar a la agencia?

  a. Para hacer las reservas.

  b. Para confirmar sus reservas.

  c. Para hacer unas preguntas.

6. ¿Cuál es el número de teléfono de la agencia?

  a. 667-2245   **b.** 267-3245   **c.** 667-3245

Después de escuchar

3-40 Planeamos el viaje. Help Elena and Teresa plan their trip. Use the names of the cities and the following verbs to express a few of the things they plan to do while in Peru.

alquilar	cenar	nadar
bailar	conversar	tomar el sol
cantar	descansar	ver

MODELO: *Teresa y Elena van a cenar en un restaurante en Lima.*

1. _____

2. _____

3. _____

A conversar

3-41   La fiesta de cumpleaños. You are planning a birthday party for your roommate, and you want to make sure that your friends from your Spanish class will be there. You call to invite some of them, but get the answering machine. Leave a message orally and tell them about the party. Give them information about the location, the food you are going to eat and the drinks you are going to have. Remember to include the details of the fun activities that will be happening.

A leer

Antes de leer

3-42   De vacaciones. Briefly look at the following article about Lima, Peru, in exercise 3-43 and answer the questions.

1. ¿Dónde aparece este artículo?
   a. en una revista de negocios
   b. en una revista de viajes
   c. en una revista de cocina

2. ¿Cuál es la función principal del artículo?
   a. informar a los turistas de las actividades posibles en esta ciudad
   b. avisar de los peligros que hay en esta ciudad
   c. describir las comidas más populares en esta ciudad

Leer

3-43   ¿Qué hacemos en Lima? Read the statements below. Then read the article about Lima and indicate whether the sentences are true (**Cierto**) or false (**Falso**).

Lima: Una ciudad fascinante

Lima es una ciudad fascinante, con muchas actividades para adultos y niños. Esta ciudad ofrece al turista muchas actividades culturales, de turismo arqueológico y de turismo de aventura. Es imposible aburrirse en Lima.

Oferta cultural:

- Caminar por la Plaza de las Armas
- Admirar la Catedral de Lima
- Ver la Iglesia y Convento de San Francisco
- Ir a las casonas: la casa Aliaga y la casa Goyoneche
- Visitar el Museo de la Nación
- Ir al Palacio de TorreTagle
- Ver la ciudad prehispánica de Caral
- Visitar Machu Picchu y las otras zonas arqueológicas
- Visitar el santuario Pachacamac
- Visitar el Palacio del Gobierno
- Ver el Tribunal del Santo Oficio

Para los niños:

- Visitar el Zoológico: Parque las Leyendas, donde la familia puede (*can*) ver los animales exóticos y los parques: El Parque Universitario y Pantanos de Villa
- Visitar las playas y balnearios: Pulpos, El Silencio, Punta Hermosa y Punta Rocas
- Ir al Museo Nacional de Arqueología, Antropología e Historia

Turismo arquelógico: Ir a Machu Picchu, la fortaleza de Sacsayhuaman, Ollantaytambo y el Camino Inca

Turismo de aventura: Para los jóvenes y los amantes (*lovers*) de experiencias intensas, hay muchas posibilidades: ciclismo de montaña en la Reserva de Paracas, andinismo en la Cordillera Blanca, surfing en Cabo Blanco

Artesanías: Visitar el Mercado en la Plaza de Armas, en el centro de la ciudad

Restaurantes:

Brujas de cachiche	Comida peruana y criolla
Vivaldino	Comida internacional

Hoteles:

Hotel Grand Bolívar	Hotel de 5☆ tradición cosmopolita
Hotel Basadre	4☆ experiencia y tradición

---

1. No es buena idea ir con niños a Lima porque no hay actividades para los niños.   Cierto   Falso

2. En esta ciudad se puede visitar las antiguas casonas.   Cierto   Falso

3. En el Parque las Leyendas los niños pueden aprender y divertirse.   Cierto   Falso

4. En Lima se puede comer comidas de otros países.   Cierto   Falso

5. La Plaza de Armas no está en el centro de la ciudad.   Cierto   Falso

6. Para tomar el sol es buena idea visitar El Silencio.   Cierto   Falso

Después de leer

3-44   De viaje. You are planning to go to Peru on vacation with a friend. She asks you what types of activities you like to do so that she can start planning the trip. Answer your friend's questions in complete sentences.

1. ¿Te gustan los museos? ¿Qué tipo de arte te gusta más?

   _____

2. ¿Te gusta caminar, o vamos a alquilar un coche?

   _____

3. ¿Te gustan las aventuras, o prefieres las actividades tranquilas? ¿Qué tipo de actividades te gustan más?

   _____

4. ¿Te gusta probar (*try*) comidas nuevas?

   _____

A escribir

Antes de escribir

3-45   A planear. The following is another list of activities you can do in Lima and the places where you can stay and eat. Write down the ones that interest you most.

Destinos

La ciudad prehispánica de Caral	El Palacio del Gobierno
Iglesia y Convento de San Francisco	La playa y los balnearios
El plaza de Armas	La catedral
El Museo de la Nación	Machu Picchu
El Palacio de TorreTagle	el Zoológico: Parque las Leyendas
La Casa Aliaga	El Parque Universitario
La Casa Goyoneche	El ciclismo de montaña en la Reserva de Paracas

Hoteles

Hotel Basadre

Double Tree el Pardo

Hotel el Ducado

Hotel Grand Bolívar

Plaza del Bosque

Delfines Hotel y Casino

Restaurantes

José Antonio – comida criolla

Señorio de Sulco – comida peruana

Zeño Manuel – comida criolla

Vivaldino – comida internacional

Costa Verde – pescados y mariscos

_____

_____

Escribir

3-46   Vacaciones fantásticas. You are spending two weeks in Peru with your friend. Write a postcard to a classmate in your Spanish class. Tell him/her where you are staying and your plans for the next few days. Use **Querido/a** + name, followed by colon (e.g., **Querida Ana a:**) to address your friend, and use **Un saludo cariñoso de** + your name as a closing.

Después de escribir

3-47   De vuelta. You and your friend just returned from Lima, Peru. Match each name with the correct description of the type of place it is, referring back as necessary to the reading about Lima in activity **3-43**.

1. _____ de la Nación
2. _____ Ollantaytambo
3. _____ Pulpos
4. _____ Plaza de Armas
5. _____ Parque las Leyendas
6. _____ San Francisco

a. playa
b. mercado
c. museo
d. iglesia
e. zoológico
f. zona arqueológica

ENFOQUE CULTURAL

3-48   Breve perfil de Perú. Reread the *Enfoque cultural* section on pages 118–119 in your textbook and indicate if the following statements are true (**Cierto**) or false (**Falso**).

1. Perú y México son las regiones más importantes durante la época colonial de América Latina.	Cierto	Falso
2. La geografía de Perú tiene tres regiones distintas: la costa, la sierra y la selva.	Cierto	Falso
3. En Perú no hay mucha diversidad étnica.	Cierto	Falso
4. La antigua capital del imperio inca es Machu Picchu.	Cierto	Falso
5. Los tres virreinatos en el continente americano durante la colonia son Perú, México y Colombia.	Cierto	Falso
6. La cultura peruana es el resultado de la mezcla de muchas culturas.	Cierto	Falso

3-49   Los restaurantes peruanos. Visit the *Mosaicos* webpage to find out more information about restaurants in Peru, and write down the names of some of the typical dishes you might eat while on vacation there.

entrada: _____

plato principal: _____

postre: _____

bebida: _____

REPASO

3-50   La comida y las bebidas. Teresa and Elena enjoy going out and eating in different restaurants and cafés. Write a list of foods and drinks that they might enjoy for breakfast, lunch, and dinner.

Desayuno: _____

_____

_____

_____

Almuerzo: _____

_____

_____

_____

Cena: _____

_____

_____

_____

3-51   El cumpleaños de Teresa. Teresa's birthday is this weekend, and Elena is planning several special activities to celebrate. Imagine that you are Elena, and write an e-mail to Teresa including the following information:

• the reason for the celebration

• where you are going to celebrate

• three sentences explaining what you and Teresa are going to do

• where both of you are going to eat

• what you are going to eat

A: teresarivera@aol.com
De: Elenita@netserve.com
Asunto: ¡Tu cumpleaños!

3-52   La fiesta de cumpleaños. Teresa and her friends are at a restaurant to celebrate her birthday. Listen to the questions and then choose the most logical answer to complete the sentences below.

1. Javier va a comer...

   a. un postre.   **b.** pollo frito.   **c.** una ensalada.

2. Teresa va a tomar...

   a. un refresco.   **b.** leche.   **c.** té.

3. Elena va a tomar...

   a. una coca-cola.   **b.** vino.   **c.** leche.

4. Juan va a comer...

   a. una hamburguesa.   **b.** pollo frito.   **c.** espaguetis.

5. _____ sirve (*serves*) la comida.

   a. Elena   **b.** El camarero   **c.** Un compañero

3-53   Vamos a preparar flan. Elena and Teresa decide to make *flan*, a typical dessert in Hispanic countries. Read the recipe for *flan* below. Then read the statements and select whether they are true (**Cierto**) or false (**Falso**).

Flan

½ litro de leche
4 huevos
200 gramos de azúcar (*sugar*)
1 cucharada (*tablespoon*) de vainilla

Primero, debes calentar (*heat*) 50 gramos de azúcar en un recipiente para hacer un almíbar (*syrup*). Segundo, necesitas poner al fuego (*put on the burner*) la leche y un poco de vainilla. Mientras se calienta la leche, debes poner y mezclar (*mix*) el resto del azúcar con los huevos. Después, es necesario añadir (*add*) la leche con los huevos y el azúcar al recipiente donde está el almíbar. Ahora necesitas poner el flan en el horno (*oven*) por 35 a 45 minutos. Cuando el flan está listo, debes ponerlo en un plato.

---

1. El flan es un postre dulce.   Cierto   Falso

2. Para preparar flan, necesitas media botella de vainilla.   Cierto   Falso

3. La leche debe estar fría cuando la mezclas (*you mix it*) con los huevos.   Cierto   Falso

4. Necesitas mezclar 150 gramos de azúcar con los huevos.   Cierto   Falso

5. El flan tiene que estar en el horno por más de (*more than*) media hora.   Cierto   Falso

Nombre: _____

Fecha: _____

En familia

4-1 ¿Quién es? Match the following descriptions with the correct members of the family.

1. _____ hija de mis padres   **a.** tío

2. _____ hermano de mi padre   **b.** abuela

3. _____ hijos de mis hijos   **c.** primos

4. _____ madre de mi madre   **d.** hermana

5. _____ hijos de mis tíos   **e.** nietos

4-2 La familia de Julieta. Using the information from Julieta's family tree, complete the following sentences.

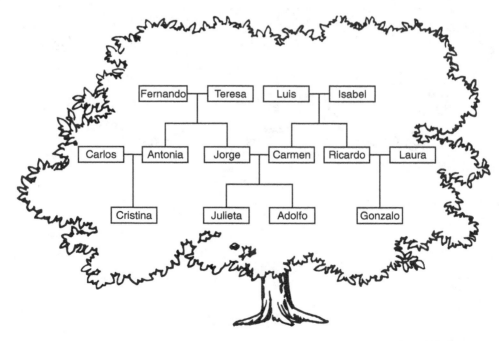

1. Fernando es el _____ de Julieta.

2. Cristina y Adolfo son _____.

3. Ricardo es el _____ de Julieta.

4. Carmen es la _____ de Adolfo.

5. Cristina es la _____ de Jorge.

6. Adolfo es el_____ de Luis.

7. Julieta y Adolfo son _____.

8. Antonia es la_____ de Adolfo.

4-3   Los parientes de Julieta. Now you will hear a series of words identifying the relationships of some of the family members to Julieta. Listen carefully to the words, and then write the name of each corresponding person. If more than one person has the same relationship to Julieta, write one of the possible names.

MODELO: You hear: abuelo

You write: *Luis*

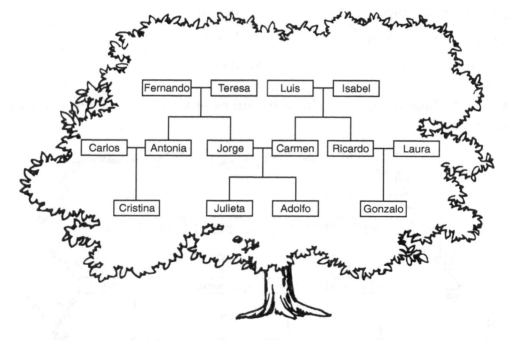

1. _____   5. _____

2. _____   6. _____

3. _____   7. _____

4. _____

4-4 Más sobre la familia de Julieta. Listen to the description of some of Julieta's family members, and then select all the relatives that are mentioned.

abuela	abuelo
hermana	hermano
madre	padre
primo	sobrina
tía	tío

4-5 Los famosos. Indicate the kind of relationship the following famous people share. If you are not sure who some of these people are, try looking them up on your favorite search engine.

MODELO: Mary Kate Olsen y Ashley Olsen   *hermanas*

1. Julio Iglesias y Enrique Iglesias   _____ e _____
2. Charlie Sheen y Emilio Estévez   _____
3. Marc Anthony y Jennifer López   _____
4. Michael Jackson y Janet Jackson   _____
5. La reina (*queen*) de Inglaterra y el príncipe William _____ y _____

4-6 ¿Y cómo es su familia? Is your family similar to or different from Julieta's? Listen to the following questions and answer in complete sentences.

MODELO: ¿Cómo se llama su tía?

  Mi tía se llama Lina.

1. _____
2. _____
3. _____
4. _____
5. _____
6. _____
7. _____
8. _____

4-7 Su familia. Now describe your family orally. Be sure to mention the name of each family member, his/her age, and his/her relationship to other family members. Also, if you are describing brothers and sisters, be sure to mention whether the person is the oldest or the youngest.

4-8 El bautizo. Read the statements below, and then listen to the description of the baptism of a new member of the Orjuela family. Finally, indicate whether each statement is **Cierto**, **Falso**, or **No dice** (not given in the passage).

1. Los Orjuela van a celebrar el bautizo de su hijo.   Cierto   Falso   No dice
2. La hermana del bebé se llama Ana María.   Cierto   Falso   No dice
3. El niño se llama Adolfo José como su padrino.   Cierto   Falso   No dice
4. Los abuelos van a ser los padrinos.   Cierto   Falso   No dice
5. El bautizo va a ser en una iglesia (*church*).   Cierto   Falso   No dice
6. El bautizo es a las seis de la tarde.   Cierto   Falso   No dice
7. Sólo la familia va al bautizo.   Cierto   Falso   No dice

4-9 Las familias de Julieta y Eduardo. You will hear Julieta García and Eduardo Orjuela, two college students from Bogotá, describing their families. Before listening, try to anticipate which relatives might be mentioned. Then listen once to get the gist of the passage. Now, look at the following charts about these families and identify the information that is missing. Finally, fill in the blanks with the information you hear.

LA FAMILIA DE JULIETA

NOMBRE	RELACIÓN	¿CÓMO ES?
1. Jorge	_____	_____
2. _____	_____	listo
3. _____	_____	conversadora
4. Antonia	_____	_____
5. _____	primo	divertido

LA FAMILIA DE EDUARDO

NOMBRE	RELACIÓN	¿CÓMO ES?
6. Ernesto	_____	_____
7. _____	madre	ocupada
8. Pedro	_____	_____
9. _____	_____	trabajadora
10. Leonor	_____	_____

4-10   La familia. Locate the following words related to families and family life in the puzzle. Be sure to look for words horizontally, vertically, diagonally and backwards.

bautizo	hijo	nieto
esposa	madre	sobrino
hermana	parientes	

e	i	t	b	e	m	p	i	i	r
o	n	p	m	o	a	a	r	s	j
s	a	o	i	a	m	r	d	o	h
r	s	n	o	r	o	i	t	r	e
o	o	d	a	z	n	e	r	r	e
o	p	h	j	m	i	n	r	u	t
s	s	a	i	n	r	t	a	n	e
d	e	a	r	j	b	e	u	a	o
n	t	t	p	t	o	s	h	a	s
u	i	o	s	a	s	u	i	r	b

EN ACCIÓN

4-11   Antes de ver. In this video segment, Javier will join Luciana and her family for a day in the park. Based on the photo from the video clip, make a list of some of the family members that might be present.

_____

_____

_____

_____

4-12   Mientras ve. As you watch the video segment, choose the answer that best completes each sentence.

1. _____ no quiere bromas hoy.
   a. Marcos   **b.** Javier   **c.** Luciana

2. Generalmente Javier duerme hasta _____.
   a. las doce   **b.** la una   **c.** las dos

3. Cuando Javier llega, hace _____ que la familia de Luciana ya está en el parque.
   a. 15 minutos   **b.** media hora   **c.** una hora

4. La madre de Luciana piensa servir la comida a _____.
   a. las doce   **b.** la una   **c.** las dos

5. Hace _____ que Javier está en México.
   a. tres días   **b.** tres semanas   **c.** tres meses

6. La abuela hace una broma con _____.
   a. la torta   **b.** la ensalada   **c.** el guacamole

4-13   Después de ver. Do you remember what everyone said? Read the following statements and write the name of the person to which each statement applies.

Javier   Luciana   Marcos   Papá   Abuela

1. Promete (*Promises*) no hacer bromas durante el almuerzo. _____

2. Dice que Javier se tiene que bañar en guacamole. _____

3. Prefiere almorzar tarde. _____

4. Dice que su familia tiene muchas tradiciones. _____

5. Pregunta si Javier piensa volver a comer con ellos. _____

FUNCIONES Y FORMAS

1. Expressing opinions, plans, preferences, and feelings: Present tense of stem-changing verbs: $e \rightarrow ie$, $o \rightarrow ue$, and $e \rightarrow i$ (Textbook p. 132)

4-14 **¿Quién es?** Eduardo is from Colombia, but this year he is studying in the United States. Listen to him talk about some things he and other people (including you) do at college. Indicate whether his statements refer to himself (*yo*), you (*tú*), his roommate Marcos, both Marcos and himself (*Marcos y yo*), or his friends (*mis amigos*).

      a. yo   **b.** tú   **c.** Marcos   **d.** Marcos y yo   **e.** mis amigos

1. _____   **5.** _____

2. _____   **6.** _____

3. _____   **7.** _____

4. _____   **8.** _____

4-15 **La rutina de Eduardo.** Although many of Eduardo's daily activities are still the same in the United States, his routine has changed in some ways. Listen to Eduardo and indicate whether the following statements refer to his life in Colombia, in the United States, or both (*los dos*).

1. Eduardo no entiende todo en clase.

    Colombia   Estados Unidos   los dos

2. Las clases empiezan muy temprano.

    Colombia   Estados Unidos   los dos

3. Eduardo duerme ocho horas.

    Colombia   Estados Unidos   los dos

4. Eduardo puede ir a biblioteca hasta (*until*) las doce de la noche.

    Colombia   Estados Unidos   los dos

5. Eduardo juega al fútbol.

    Colombia   Estados Unidos   los dos

4-16 Las actividades de Eduardo. Look at the following sentences, which have been taken from Eduardo's description of his activities in activity **4-15.** Then listen to him again and complete the sentences with the missing verbs.

1. Mis compañeros de clase _____ explicar las cosas que son difíciles para mí.

2. En Colombia _____ ocho horas porque normalmente _____ ir a clases por la tarde.

3. En Colombia y en Estados Unidos _____ mucha tarea.

4. Casi todos los estudiantes _____ a la biblioteca y al laboratorio de computadoras; yo también _____ a la biblioteca frecuentemente.

5. Aquí los libros _____ mucho dinero.

6. En Colombia yo _____ al fútbol.

7. En Estados Unidos los jóvenes_____ el béisbol o básquetbol.

4-17 La carta a los Reyes Magos. Eduardo's five year old nephew Antonio has written a letter to the three Wise Men (*los tres Reyes Magos*), telling them the gifts (*los regalos*) he and his parents want. Help Antonio complete the letter with the correct verb forms.

Queridos Reyes Magos,

Mis amigos (1) _____ (decir) que los Reyes Magos no existen, pero yo (2) _____ (pensar) que eso es falso. Este año (3) _____ (querer) muchas cosas porque soy muy bueno. Yo (4) _____ (pedir) un auto de juguete, una bicicleta, unos libros, y unos videojuegos. (5) _____ (preferir) una bicicleta roja, por favor. También Lassie, mi perrita (*little dog*), necesita una casita. Ahora ella (6) _____ (dormir) en el jardín. Mi mamá no (7) _____ (querer) muchas cosas, pero mi papá (8) _____ (preferir) un libro y un televisor nuevo.

Bueno... pues, es todo. Gracias por los regalos. En la mesa hay leche y galletas (*cookies*).

Antonio

4-18   ¿Qué piden? Eduardo and his family enjoy eating out in different types of restaurants. Complete the following sentences about what he and each of his family members order, using the correct forms of the verb *pedir*.

MODELO: En un restaurante español, mi abuelo *pide* paella.

1. En un restaurante italiano, mi hermana _____ espaguetis.

2. En un restaurante chino, mis padres _____ arroz frito.

3. En un restaurante mexicano, todos nosotros _____ tacos.

4. En un restaurante de comida rápida, yo _____ una hamburguesa.

5. En un restaurante francés, mi tía _____ salmón.

4-19   ¿Pueden o no pueden? Indicate whether the following people can or cannot do each of these activities by completing the sentences with the correct form of the verb **poder**.

MODELOS: Bill Gates *puede* comprar una mansión o

Un niño de un año *no puede* montar en bicicleta.

1. Una persona ciega (*blind*) _____ manejar (*drive*) un auto.

2. Un bebé de tres meses _____ caminar.

3. Una persona de 90 años _____ correr diez millas.

4. Los estudiantes _____ usar la computadora.

5. Una persona con mucha responsabilidad en una compañía _____ ir de vacaciones dos meses por año.

6. Los niños de diez años _____ beber alcohol en público.

2. Expressing obligation: *Tener que + infinitive* (Textbook p. 136)

4-20   ¿Qué tenemos que hacer? Indicate where Julieta and her friends have to go or what they need to do to get what they want. Complete the following sentences with the most logical phrase from the word bank.

comprar café	ir a la librería	poner la mesa
estudiar	ir a la playa	preparar la comida

MODELO: Julieta necesita comida para la cena. Julieta *tiene que ir al supermercado*.

1. Julieta quiere comprar un libro. Julieta _____.

2. Eduardo quiere sacar una buena nota en el examen de antropología. Eduardo

_____.

3. Marcos quiere cenar lasaña. Marcos _____.

4. Yo quiero tomar café con leche. Yo _____.

5. Marcos y Eduardo quieren servir la cena. Ellos _____.

6. Julieta quiere tomar el sol. Julieta _____.

4-21   ¿Qué tienen que hacer? Eduardo is working as a Resident Assistant in the university residence halls this semester, and the students always have a lot of questions. Help Eduardo answer them by reading the questions below and completing the sentences with the actions that students have to take.

comer bien y hacer ejercicio	hablar con él	sacar su pasaporte
comprar nuevos discos compactos	practicar	tomar el autobús

MODELO: Juan: Estoy muy preocupado porque saco muy malas notas en la universidad. Quiero sacar muy buenas notas, pero me gusta mirar televisión y jugar al golf. Los fines de semana voy a fiestas. ¿Qué puedo hacer?

Juan *tiene que estudiar más.*

1. Ernesto: Tengo problemas de salud y quiero bajar de peso, pero me gusta mucho comer hamburguesas y papas fritas para el almuerzo. Por la tarde tomo helado con mis amigos. Nunca corro, y no me gusta hacer ejercicio. ¿Qué puedo hacer?

Ernesto _____.

2. Elena: Soy una muchacha norteamericana, pero tengo parientes en Cali, Colombia. Voy a ir a Colombia durante mis vacaciones, y voy a pasar dos semanas con mis parientes. Es mi primer viaje al extranjero (*abroad*).

Elena _____,

3. Michael: Juego en una competencia muy importante de fútbol americano la próxima semana. Mis amigos y yo estamos muy nerviosos porque queremos ganar (*win*). ¿Qué hacemos?

Michael y sus amigos _____.

4. Amparo: Tengo un MP3 nuevo para escuchar música. La música que tengo está pasada de moda (*outdated*), y mis amigos van a venir a mi casa esta tarde. ¿Qué hago?

Amparo _____.

5. Mario: Estoy enfadado (*angry*) con mi compañero de cuarto. Cuando yo tengo que estudiar, él habla por teléfono. Nunca estudia, y siempre tiene muchos amigos en el cuarto. ¿Qué puedo hacer?

Mario _____.

6. Rebeca: Tengo un trabajo muy bueno, pero está muy lejos de mi casa. Normalmente voy al trabajo en mi auto, pero en estos días no funciona (*it is not working*). ¿Qué puedo hacer?

Rebeca _____.

4-22 Las obligaciones de Eduardo. Eduardo writes a postcard telling his family how busy he and his roommate are. Complete the paragraph with phrases that express their obligations.

Hola a todos:

Estoy bien, pero muy ocupado. Tengo tres exámenes esta semana; entonces yo _____. Marcos quiere jugar fútbol en el equipo de la universidad; entonces él _____. Las cosas aquí cuestan mucho y nosotros no tenemos mucho dinero. Si queremos comprar discos compactos y otras cosas, nosotros _____ Finalmente, ¡la comida es deliciosa! Como mucho y necesito perder peso... _____

_____

Un abrazo para todos,

Eduardo

4-23 ¿Y usted? You are also very busy and have a lot of obligations. You realize that you cannot complete this week's homework, so you call your professor to ask for an extension on the due date. Leave him/her a message and explain all the things you have to do this week.

3. Expressing when, where, or how an action occurs: Adverbs (Textbook p. 138)

🔊)) **4-24   Antonio conversa con su tío.** Antonio is very close to his uncle Eduardo, and they often call each other while Eduardo is in the United States. Listen to a portion of a conversation between the two of them. Then select the word that best completes each statement.

1. Eduardo tiene clase de guitarra…

   a. semanalmente.   **b.** diariamente.   **c.** raramente.

2. Eduardo practica la guitarra…

   a. semanalmente.   **b.** diariamente.   **c.** raramente.

3. Eduardo y sus compañeros practican por dos horas…

   a. normalmente.   **b.** lentamente.   **c.** raramente.

4. Eduardo y sus compañeros tocan…

   a. muy bien.   **b.** regular.   **c.** muy mal.

5. Eduardo va a la biblioteca…

   a. lentamente.   **b.** tranquilamente.   **c.** rápidamente.

6. Eduardo hace la tarea primero, y puede comer…

   a. mañana.   **b.** mientras.   **c.** después.

🔊)) **4-25   Antonio y su tío siguen la conversación.** You will hear Antonio asking Eduardo some questions. Read Eduardo's answers below, and write the number of each question next to the appropriate answer.

_____ Mañana, Antonio… te llamo mañana.

_____ Porque generalmente no tengo tiempo para practicar.

_____ Me gusta, pero realmente prefiero la guitarra.

_____ Sí, toco el piano, pero no frecuentemente.

_____ Toco mal, porque no practico mucho.

4-26   ¿Cómo lo hacen? Complete the sentences to indicate how the following people or objects perform certain actions.

MODELO: Las personas tímidas hablan *nerviosamente* en público.

1. Los políticos honestos hablan _____.

2. Los autos modernos corren _____.

3. Para ir a una recepción formal, el ejecutivo viste _____.

4. Las personas pacíficas resuelven los problemas _____.

5. Las personas positivas viven _____.

4-27   Mi mundo. Everyone experiences the world differently. Complete the following sentences with an adverb that best describes your personal experience.

1. Me gusta comer _____.

2. Mi autor favorito escribe _____.

3. Los profesores de mi universidad visten _____.

4. Por lo general, analizo los problemas _____.

5. Prefiero viajar _____.

6. Yo resuelvo los problemas _____.

7. En público hablo _____.

8. Manejo (*I drive*) mi auto _____.

4-28 En la universidad. A reporter for the school newspaper is writing an article about the routines of university students. Think of your daily life as a student, and answer the reporter's questions. Choose from the adjectives in the list and make them adverbs, or think of your own adverbs to answer the questions.

básico	frecuente	lento	relativo	simple
fácil	general	rápido	regular	tranquilo

MODELO: ¿Cómo desayunas? *Desayuno tranquilamente.*

1. ¿Cuándo estudias?_____

2. ¿Cómo manejas?_____

3. ¿Cómo caminas?_____

4. ¿Cómo hablas?_____

5. ¿Cómo trabajas?_____

4. Expressing how long something has been going on: *Hace* with expressions of time (Textbook p. 140)

🔊 **4-29   ¿Cuánto tiempo hace?** You will hear Eduardo describe his nephew Antonio and his activities. Before listening to the description, look at the sentences below. Then, as you listen, complete the sentences with the correct amount of time.

MODELO: La familia de Antonio vive en Bogotá *hace*

cinco años.

1. Antonio vive en esa casa _____.
2. Estudia en la Escuela Moderna _____.
3. Antonio y Pablito son amigos _____.
4. Antonio tiene su bicicleta _____.
5. Tiene un perro (*dog*) _____.

🔊 **4-30   ¡Cuánto tiempo!** Read the questions below and then listen to the conversation between Julieta and her aunt Laura. Finally, fill in the blanks with the correct amount of time.

1. ¿Cuánto tiempo hace que Julieta no ve a su tía Laura?
   Hace _____.
2. ¿Cuánto tiempo hace que Julieta estudia en la universidad?
   Hace _____.
3. ¿Cuánto tiempo hace que Gonzalo toca la guitarra?
   Hace _____.
4. ¿Cuánto tiempo hace que Gonzalo toma clases de piano?
   Hace _____.

4-31   Las actividades de su familia. Your family is involved in a number of activities. Describe how long each person has been doing their chosen activity by writing the sentence fragments in the correct order. Be sure to begin your sentences with the capitalized word.

MODELO: cinco/que/Hace/meses/veo/a mi prima Patricia

Hace cinco meses que veo a mi prima Patricia.

1. mi hermana/que/juega/años/al voleibol/Hace/tres

_____

2. español/que estudio/un/año/Hace

_____

3. viven en/Mis padres/hace/diez/años/nuestra casa

_____

4. tu coche/nuevo/hace/Cuánto/tienes/que/tiempo

¿_____?

5. Tengo/mi coche/nuevo/años/tres/hace

_____

4-32   ¿Cuánto tiempo hace que... ? Your cousin, whom you have not seen for a long time, is visiting you. You are catching up on all you have or have not done since you saw each other last. Write complete sentences, saying how long you have been doing each activity.

MODELO: jugar tenis

Hace dos años que juego tenis. o

Juego tenis hace dos años. o

No juego tenis, pero hace un año que juego fútbol con el equipo de la universidad.

1. hacer ejercicio: _____

2. ser estudiante: _____

3. estudiar español: _____

4. tener novio/a: _____

5. tomar café: _____

6. manejar un auto: _____

5. Talking about daily routines: Reflexive verbs and pronouns (Textbook p. 142)

4-33   Dos hermanos diferentes. Julieta and Adolfo are brother and sister, but they do not have the same habits. Read the questions, and then listen to the passage in which Julieta talks about herself and her brother. Finally, indicate whether the information refers to Julieta, Adolfo, or both (*los dos*).

1. ¿Quién se levanta a las siete?	Julieta	Adolfo	los dos
2. ¿Quién duerme hasta las once los fines de semana?	Julieta	Adolfo	los dos
3. ¿Quién come cereal?	Julieta	Adolfo	los dos
4. ¿Quién no desayuna siempre?	Julieta	Adolfo	los dos
5. ¿Quién se viste rápidamente?	Julieta	Adolfo	los dos
6. ¿Quién se baña y se viste lentamente?	Julieta	Adolfo	los dos
7. ¿Quién duerme por lo menos (*at least*) siete horas?	Julieta	Adolfo	los dos

4-34   Un día en la vida de Julieta. In this e-mail to you, Julieta talks about her daily activities as well as those of her parents. Complete it by filling in the blanks with the correct reflexive pronouns.

¡Hola!

En mi familia, todos estamos muy ocupados y generalmente (1) _____ levantamos muy temprano. A las siete de la mañana suena el despertador y yo (2) _____ despierto. En mi casa, mi padre (3) _____ baña primero; luego mi madre (4) _____ ducha y (5) _____ seca con una toalla. Yo (6) _____ visto en mi dormitorio. En la noche, yo (7) _____ acuesto temprano y mis padres (8) _____ acuestan más tarde. Todos (9) _____ dormimos antes de las doce. ¿Y tú? ¿A qué hora (10) _____ acuestas? ¿Cómo es la rutina diaria de tu familia?

4-35   ¿Qué hacen por la mañana? Your instructor has asked you to write a composition about the daily routines of your family members. Prepare the set of questions below for each person by completing them with the correct form of the verbs in parentheses. Be sure to address them informally (*tú*).

1. ¿A qué hora (levantarse) _____?

2. ¿Cuándo (bañarse) _____?

3. ¿Cuándo (vestirse) _____?

4. ¿ _____ (acostarse) temprano todos los días?

4-36 Mi prima Cristina. In another email, Julieta tells you about her cousin Cristina and what she usually does during the day. Complete the following paragraph with the correct forms of the verbs from the list.

acostarse	levantarse
dormirse	vestirse
ducharse	

Cristina (1) _____ tarde, como a las nueve o las diez de la mañana. Después (2) _____ y se seca. Ella es modelo, y siempre (3) _____ con ropa elegante porque tiene que practicar para sus desfiles. Después de un día de trabajo largo, Cristina llega a casa muy tarde y (4) _____ inmediatamente. A Cristina le gusta leer las revistas de moda en cama. Después de leer por una hora o dos, (5) _____.

4-37 La rutina diaria. You finally have time to write back to Julieta and answer her questions about your family. Write an email and tell her all about your routine as well as the daily activities of at least two other members of your family.

_____

_____

_____

_____

_____

MOSAICOS

A escuchar

Antes de escuchar

4-38   Una visita al museo. You are visiting friends in Bogotá, Colombia, and one of them wants to take you to a museum. Look at your agenda to check the activities you have already planned for tomorrow, and write down below, in digits, the times that you are *not* available. Be sure to write them in order.

```
miércoles, 3 de octubre
   9:00   Desayuno con Marina.
  10:00   _____
  11:00   _____
  12:00   _____
   1:00   _____
   2:00   Como con Mirella y su familia.
   3:00   Hago compras con Mirella.
   4:00   _____
   5:00   _____
   6:00   _____
```

1. _____   2. _____   3. _____

Escuchar

4-39   El mensaje. Listen to the message from your friend Verónica and write down what she is doing tomorrow at each of the times you are free. If she does not mention any activity for a particular time, write nada (*nothing*). Finally, complete the statement with the time that you are able to go, remembering that you will need two hours at the museum.

MODELO: You see: 10:00
              You hear: Yo tengo una clase de inglés a las diez.
              You write: *clase de inglés*

1. 11:00 _____   5. 5:00 _____
2. 12:00 _____   6. 6:00 _____
3. 1:00 _____   7. Podemos ir al museo a la(s) _____
4. 4:00 _____   de la tarde.

Después de escuchar

4-40   ¿Qué información necesitas? Listen to your friend's message again and complete the sentences with the information you need.

1. El museo se llama Museo _____.

2. Está en la calle _____.

3. Cuesta _____ pesos para los estudiantes.

A conversar

4-41   ¡Vamos al museo! You call Verónica and reach her voice mail. Leave a message, telling her how long it has been since you have visited a museum and that you really want to go. Talk about your schedule for the day, and let her know what time you are able to go to the museum.

A leer

Antes de leer

4-42   ¿Cómo se titula? Read the first two lines of the following article.

1. Which of the following would be the best title for it?

   a. La Fundación Amor y Paz: Casa y dinero para las familias pobres

   b. La Fundación Amor y Paz: Guardería para niños pobres

   c. La Fundación Amor y Paz: Gran ayuda para familias de recursos limitados

Leer

4-43   La Fundación Amor y Paz. Read the following article about a Colombian couple that started a nonprofit organization in Cali. Then indicate whether the statements that follow are **Cierto, Falso,** or **No dice** (not mentioned in the article).

En la ciudad de Cali vive una pareja joven que se dedica a ayudar (*help*) a las familias pobres. Ayudan a los padres a buscar trabajo y mantienen una guardería (*day-care center*) gratis para los niños.

Este joven matrimonio es muy respetado y admirado en la ciudad. El hombre, Camilo Gómez Buendía, licenciado (*graduated*) en ciencias económicas, decidió dejar (*quit*) su carrera para comenzar esta labor. Su esposa, Mónica Jaramillo de Gómez, es su compañera de trabajo. El padre de Mónica, el conocido periodista (*well-known journalist*) Fernando Jaramillo Torres, publicó (*published*) un artículo sobre esta organización, y la reacción fue (*was*) extraordinaria. Hoy en día la Fundación Amor y Paz ayuda a más de cien familias a rehacer su vida.

Mónica es la tercera (*third*) hija del matrimonio Jaramillo. Ella y su madre, Blanca Giraldo de Jaramillo, entrevistan a las familias y con psicólogos y voluntarios ofrecen ayuda a las familias que la necesitan. Los hijos de Camilo y Mónica, de tres y cinco años, participan en los juegos y actividades de la guardería. De esta forma, toda la familia contribuye al trabajo de la Fundación.

1. La Fundación Amor y Paz ofrece (*offers*) casas para las familias de recursos limitados.	Cierto	Falso	No dice
2. La guardería de la fundación cuesta mucho dinero.	Cierto	Falso	No dice
3. La hermana de Camilo también trabaja en la fundación.	Cierto	Falso	No dice
4. Las primas de Mónica también trabajan en la guardería.	Cierto	Falso	No dice
5. La madre de Mónica coopera en la fundación.	Cierto	Falso	No dice
6. La fundación busca trabajo para las familias que lo necesitan.	Cierto	Falso	No dice
7. Camilo y Mónica no tienen hijos.	Cierto	Falso	No dice
8. El padre de Mónica es psicólogo y ayuda a entrevistar a las familias.	Cierto	Falso	No dice

Después de leer

4-44   ¿Qué más? Do you know of any organization(s) similar to *La Fundación Amor y Paz*? What programs might they be able to offer in addition to the ones they already offer? List three suggestions below.

1. _____

2. _____

3. _____

A escribir

Antes de escribir

4-45   Ayuda. You have volunteered to be a pen pal for one of the young people receiving help from the Foundation. You will write him/her a letter to introduce yourself, but first you should brainstorm. Make a list of interesting facts about yourself and your family: who you are, what you do, and the activities or hobbies you enjoy.

_____

_____

_____

_____

_____

Escribir

4-46   Primer contacto. Now write a letter introducing yourself to your new Colombian pen-pal. Tell him/her about yourself. Describe your family and mention what your daily routine is like.

_____

_____

_____

_____

_____

_____

_____

_____

_____

_____

_____

_____

Después de escribir

4-47   Una llamada telefónica. The volunteers at the foundation have arranged for you and your new pen-pal to speak on the telephone. Think of all the things you would like to know about him/her, his/her family and about Colombia. Write your list of questions below, to prepare for the phone conversation.

_____

_____

_____

_____

_____

_____

ENFOQUE CULTURAL

4-48   La riqueza de Colombia. Read the *Enfoque cultural* section on pages 150–152 in your textbook again, and then select the most appropriate answer to each of the following questions.

1. Juan Valdéz es...
   a. el presidente de Colombia.
   b. el representante de Colombia ante (*to*) el mundo.
   c. una imagen corporativa asociada con el café.

2. Colombia es el único país que tiene...
   a. costas en los dos mares.
   b. playas espectaculares.
   c. selvas tropicales.

3. La Amazonía colombiana...
   a. es la región con más biodiversidad.
   b. es famosa por tener gente de un carácter alegre.
   c. produce una gran cantidad de oxígeno.

4. Colombia y _____ forman la región de los Llanos Orientales.
   a. Perú   b. Venezuela   c. Brasil

5. El mejor café en Colombia se produce en...
   a. Bogotá.   b. Armenia.   c. Medellín.

6. La mayoría de los habitantes viven en...
   a. la zona tropical.   b. la capital.   c. la zona central.

7. La isla de San Andrés es el lugar ideal para...
   a. una reserva natural.   b. el turismo.   c. una universidad.

4-49   La familia de Fernando Botero. At the beginning of this chapter, you learned about the paintings of the famous Colombian artist Fernando Botero. Now visit the *Mosaicos* webpage to read Botero's biography. Look for information about his family and write the names of the family members mentioned in his biography.

RELACIÓN	NOMBRE
padre	1. _____
madre	2. _____
tío	3. _____
hermanos	4. _____
	5. _____

REPASO

4-50   La familia de Pablo. Use Pablo's family tree to complete the following descriptions of the members of his family.

don José   doña Olga

María   Jorge   Lola   Elena   Jaime

Elenita   Ana   Jorgito   Sofía   Inés   Pablo

1. Elena es la _____ de Jorgito.

2. Lola y Elena son _____.

3. Inés y Jorgito son _____.

4. Jorgito es el _____ de don José.

5. María es la _____ de Jorge.

6. María es la _____ de Elenita.

7. Jaime es el _____ de Inés y Pablo.

8. Elena es la _____ de doña Olga.

9. Sofía es la _____ de don José.

10. Ana es la _____ de Lola.

4-51   El almuerzo en casa. Pablo has a very large family and they are all very busy, but they make time to eat lunch at home together every day. Write to Pablo and describe the members of your family. Be sure to mention the following:

- where you live and how long you have lived there
- some of the daily activities of each member of your family
- the ways in which you spend time together

4-52   El bautizo de Patricia. There will soon be a baptism in Pablo's family, and everyone is preparing for this special day. Read the sentences that follow, and then listen to Pablo talk about the baptism. Finally select the answer that best completes each sentence.

1. Pablo va al bautizo de...

   a. su prima.   **b.** su hermana.   **c.** su sobrina.

2. El abuelo de Patricia va a ser...

   a. el sobrino.   **b.** el padre.   **c.** el padrino.

3. Los _____ de Patricia van a comprar el regalo.

   a. hermanos   **b.** abuelos   **c.** padres

4. Después de cenar, toda la familia va a...

   a. conversar.   **b.** tomar cerveza.   **c.** dormir.

5. Hace seis meses que Pablo...

   a. va de compras.   **b.** estudia y trabaja.   **c.** mira la televisión.

4-53   El mundo literario. Pablo is studying literature and enjoys reading novels about families. Below is a description of a novel written by the Spanish author Carmen Laforet. Read the text, and then indicate whether the statements that follow are **Cierto, Falso** or **No dice** (not mentioned).

Nada es la historia de Andrea, una chica que va a estudiar en Barcelona. En Barcelona, vive en un apartamento sucio (*dirty*) con su abuela, su tía Angustias, sus tíos Juan y Román, la esposa de Juan y su hijo. Como indica el título, no ocurre mucho en la novela. El énfasis es en el estado psicológico de Andrea y los cambios que ella experimenta durante un año en Barcelona. También hay paralelos entre los elementos grotescos de la novela y la situación social y política de España en la década de los años cuarenta. Andrea sufre hambre (*hunger*) en la novela, como los españoles durante esta época.

La crítica y el público piensan que es una novela muy buena. Todavía (*Still*) hoy en día, personas de todo el mundo compran y leen esta novela excepcional.

1. *Nada* es la historia de una muchacha.	Cierto	Falso	No dice
2. El hijo de Juan es muy joven.	Cierto	Falso	No dice
3. Angustias es la esposa de Román.	Cierto	Falso	No dice
4. Andrea vive en Barcelona con su abuela, sus tíos y su primo.	Cierto	Falso	No dice
5. Andrea está con su familia en Barcelona para trabajar.	Cierto	Falso	No dice
6. La novela se relaciona con la situación política de los años treinta.	Cierto	Falso	No dice
7. *Nada* es una novela popular hoy en día.	Cierto	Falso	No dice

Nombre: _____

Fecha: _____

Mi casa es su casa

A PRIMERA VISTA

5-1   ¿Dónde los pongo? You are helping a friend move into a new apartment. Match each piece of furniture, fixture or appliance with the place in the house where it should logically go.

1. _____ la cama   **a.** el dormitorio

2. _____ el sofá   **b.** la sala

3. _____ el microondas   **c.** el baño

4. _____ la barbacoa   **d.** la cocina

5. _____ la ducha   **e.** el jardín

5-2   Mi casa. Your friend Adriana is telling you about the house she is planning on renting. Complete her description with the words from the word bank.

cama	lavabo	muebles	refrigerador
chimenea	lavaplatos	piscina	sofá

La casa que voy a alquilar es grande, pero no tiene nada; no tiene (1) _____ , así que para la habitación tengo que traer mi propia (*own*) (2) _____ para poder dormir. Para la sala, traigo mi (3) _____ para sentarme (*sit*) a mirar la televisión. La cocina está completamente equipada (*equipped*). En la cocina tengo un (4) _____ para conservar la comida fría y un (5) _____ para lavar los platos después de comer. En el baño hay un (6) _____ de mármol (*marble*) para lavarme las manos. ¡Es muy bonito! Además, en la casa hay una (7) _____ para calentar la casa en el invierno. Y lo mejor de todo… en el jardín hay una gran (8) _____ donde puedo nadar con mis amigos en el verano.

5-3   ¿Qué apartamento es? Imagine that you work at the university housing center. Three messages on your answering machine describe newly available properties, one of which has been diagrammed and faxed to your office. First, look at the apartment's layout. Then listen to the three messages and identify the description that matches the apartment. Finally, complete the sentence below by writing **1, 2,** or **3.**

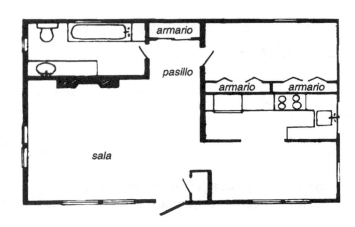

1. Este es el apartamento número _____.

5-4   El apartamento de Adriana. Your friend Adriana was not able to rent the house that she told you about, and you realize that the apartment you just reviewed (in exercise **5-3**) would be perfect for her. She likes it and decides to rent it. Now listen to Adriana, and match each piece of furniture or appliance to the room she keeps it in.

1. _____ el refrigerador   **a.** la sala

2. _____ la alfombra   **b.** el cuarto

3. _____ la mesa   **c.** la cocina

4. _____ la lavadora   **d.** el comedor

5. _____ la mesa de noche   **e.** el pasillo

5-5   Una casa para la familia Rivera. Professor Rivera and his family are also looking for a house, and one of your colleagues has good news. Read each of the statements below; then listen to him and indicate whether the statements are **Cierto, Falso** or **No dice** (the passage does not give the information).

1. Los señores Rivera quieren una casa en un barrio tranquilo.   Cierto   Falso   No dice

2. Los señores Rivera tienen siete hijas.   Cierto   Falso   No dice

3. Limpian la casa los sábados.   Cierto   Falso   No dice

4. La abuela visita a la familia a veces.   Cierto   Falso   No dice

5. La casa tiene dos pisos.   Cierto   Falso   No dice

6. Hay un garaje para tres coches.   Cierto   Falso   No dice

7. Hay cuatro dormitorios en la casa.   Cierto   Falso   No dice

8. No hay terraza, pero hay piscina.   Cierto   Falso   No dice

5-6   ¿En qué parte de la casa? You are helping the Rivera family move to their new house. The moving company is bringing all of their belongings, and the movers ask where to put each item. Listen to their questions and tell them to put each item in the room where it is usually found.

MODELO: You hear: ¿Dónde quiere la cómoda?

You say: *en el dormitorio*

1. ...   5. ...

2. ...   6. ...

3. ...   7. ...

4. ...   8. ...

5-7 Las tareas domésticas. Adriana and her new roommates have just been chosen to appear on MTV's *Room Raiders*, and the new apartment is already a mess! Use the verbs below and the vocabulary from *Capítulo 5* to make a list of all the things they need to do to get the apartment ready.

barrer	ordenar	planchar	secar
limpiar	pasar	sacar	tender

MODELO: *secar los platos*

1. _____
2. _____
3. _____
4. _____
5. _____
6. _____
7. _____
8. _____

5-8   ¿Qué deben hacer? Your friends always call you when they are in a situation in which they do not know what to do. Read your friends' dilemmas and select the most appropriate advice.

1. Su amiga tiene un día muy importante mañana. Cuando va al armario a buscar la ropa (*clothes*), ve que todo está sucio. ¿Qué debe hacer?

   a. barrer   **b.** lavar la ropa   **c.** pasar la aspiradora   **d.** comprar un lavaplatos

2. Su amigo quiere vender su apartamento. Hoy va a venir un agente y su apartamento está muy desordenado. ¿Qué debe hacer?

   a. regar las plantas   **c.** ordenar el apartamento
   b. usar el microondas   **d.** planchar la ropa

3. Su amigo va a hacer una barbacoa en el jardín esta tarde. Quiere invitarlo/la a usted y a otros amigos. ¿Qué debe hacer?

   a. secar la ropa   **b.** hacer la cama   **c.** barrer la terraza   **d.** pasar la aspiradora

4. Los abuelos de su amiga van a visitarla y van a dormir en el cuarto de ella. ¿Que debe hacer?

   a. secar la ropa   **b.** hacer la cama   **c.** barrer la terraza   **d.** regar las plantas

5. Su amiga quiere preparar una cena muy grande, pero todos los platos están sucios. ¿Qué debe hacer?

   a. regar las plantas   **c.** ordenar el apartamento
   b. usar el microondas   **d.** lavar los platos

5-9   ¿Cuándo hace las tareas domésticas? You also just moved into your own apartment, and your mother would like to know how you are handling the household chores. Write her a brief e-mail message telling her which household chores you do and how often you do them.

Hola, mamá:
_____
_____
_____
_____
_____
_____
_____
_____

5-10   Crucigrama. Complete the crossword puzzle by providing the word that correctly answers each of the following clues. All words refer to parts of the house, furniture or appliances.

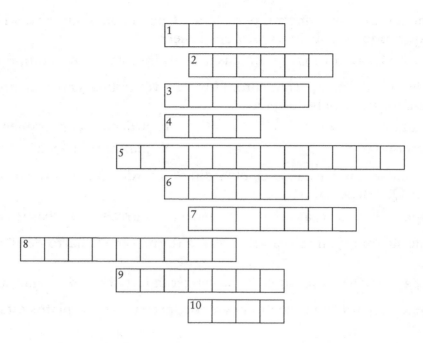

1. Podemos escuchar música y programas con este aparato.

2. Preparamos la comida en esta parte de la casa.

3. Aquí hay plantas, y los niños pueden jugar y correr. A veces también hay una piscina.

4. Usamos este mueble para dormir.

5. Es el electrodoméstico que mantiene la comida fría.

6. Es similar a una silla grande y cómoda.

7. Las personas normalmente comen en esta parte de la casa.

8. Usamos este aparato eléctrico para mirar y escuchar programas.

9. Es la decoración que ponemos en las ventanas.

10. Es el mueble donde pueden sentarse (*sit*) dos o tres personas, y normalmente está en la sala.

EN ACCIÓN

5-11   Antes de ver. In this video segment, Javier tells Daniel that he is looking for an apartment or a room to rent and they discuss the details of one that he has already seen. Before you watch the segment, look at the words below and write the name of each item under the room where you would find it.

	la ducha	el horno	el fregadero
	el sofá	el inodoro	el televisor

LA SALA	**LA COCINA**	**EL BAÑO**
1. _____	3. _____	5. _____
2. _____	4. _____	6. _____

5-12   Mientras ve. As you watch the video segment, indicate whether the following statements are **Cierto**, **Falso**, or **No dice** (the information is not given in the video clip).

1. Javier quiere alquilar un apartamento o un dormitorio por un mes.

    Cierto   Falso   No dice

2. Daniel está filmando todos los apartamentos.

    Cierto   Falso   No dice

3. A Javier le gusta un apartamento amueblado en las afueras de Coyoacán.

    Cierto   Falso   No dice

4. El apartamento tiene una terraza grande.

    Cierto   Falso   No dice

5. La señora que alquila el apartamento lo limpia bien.

    Cierto   Falso   No dice

6. Javier decide compartir la renta de un apartamento con Daniel.

    Cierto   Falso   No dice

7. Daniel guarda muchas cosas en su clóset.

    Cierto   Falso   No dice

5-13   Después de ver. Imagine that the woman in the video segment is now getting her apartment ready to show to someone else. Based on the following photos from this episode, write two sentences using the present progressive to describe what she is doing to make the apartment presentable.

MODELO: *Está ordenando el apartamento.*

1. _____

2. _____

Nombre: _____   Fecha: _____

FUNCIONES Y FORMAS

1. Expressing ongoing actions: Present progressive (Textbook p. 164)

5-14   Una nueva casa. Adriana and her friends are helping Professor Rivera and his wife get their new house in order. Read the sentences that describe what they are doing. Then complete the sentences with the present progressive form of the most logical verb from the word bank.

hacer	limpiar
barrer	pasar
cortar	

MODELO: Los hijos del profesor Rivera *están regando* las plantas.

1. Jaime _____ el césped.
2. Alicia _____ el baño.
3. El profesor Rivera _____ la terraza.
4. La señora Rivera _____ la aspiradora.
5. Adriana _____ las camas.

5-15   ¿Qué están haciendo? Read the sentences below about Professor Rivera and his wife and Adriana, Alicia, and Jaime. Based on where they are, indicate what they are probably doing.

MODELO: Jaime está en la cafetería.

Está tomando café.

1. Adriana está en la terraza.

_____

2. Alicia está en la cama.

_____

3. La señora Rivera está al lado del refrigerador.

_____

4. Jaime está en el baño.

_____

5. Adriana y Alicia están en la cocina.

_____

6. El profesor Rivera está en la sala.

_____

7. La señora Rivera está en el comedor.

_____

5-16 Una conversación por teléfono. Adriana's parents and grandparents are visiting from El Salvador. Her sister, Amanda, calls from El Salvador to find out what everyone is doing. Complete the dialogue below with the correct present progressive form of the most logical verb from the list. Use each verb only once.

dormir	estudiar	preparar	
escribir	hacer	reparar	ver

AMANDA: ¡Hola, Adriana! ¿Qué tal? ¿Qué (1) _____ ahora?

ADRIANA: ¡Hola, Amanda! Yo (2) _____ la televisión. Ponen mi telenovela favorita.

AMANDA: ¡Qué bueno! Y ¿dónde está mamá?

ADRIANA: Está en la cocina. (3) _____ un pastel para el cumpleaños de papá.

AMANDA: ¿Y papá?

ADRIANA: Está en el garaje. (4) _____ mi auto, que tiene algún problema.

AMANDA: ¡Papá es tan buen mecánico! Y tus amigos, ¿qué hacen?

ADRIANA: Alicia está en la biblioteca; (5) _____ para un examen mañana.

AMANDA: Claro, como siempre. ¿Y qué hace Jaime?

ADRIANA: Jaime (6) _____ todavía (*still*) porque anoche (*last night*) fue a una fiesta y ahora está cansado. ¿Y tú, qué haces?

AMANDA: (7) _____ un informe (*report*) para la clase de antropología. Bueno, Adriana, te dejo (*I'll let you go*) porque tengo que terminar.

ADRIANA: Bueno. Cuídate (*take care*) y llámame pronto.

5-17 La familia de Adriana. You are studying with Adriana when her sister Amanda calls again. Everyone is busy doing different things, so they cannot come to the phone. Listen to Adriana and match each activity with the name of the person who is doing it.

1. _____ Adriana   a. está sacando la basura.

2. _____ La madre   b. está lavando los platos.

3. _____ El padre   c. está estudiando para un examen.

4. _____ El abuelo   d. está conversando con un amigo.

5. _____ La abuela   e. está durmiendo en su cuarto.

5-18   Las actividades de la familia de Alicia. Alicia calls home and her father answers the phone. Read the questions that Alicia asks and then listen to the answers her father gives. Finally, write the complete sentence giving the correct information.

MODELO: You see: ¿Mamá está lavando los platos?

→ If you hear: Sí, es verdad.

You write: *Mamá está lavando los platos.*

→ If you hear: No, Mamá está pasando la aspiradora.

You write: *Mamá está pasando la aspiradora.*

1. Papá, ¿estás mirando la televisión?

_____

2. ¿Clara está estudiando?

_____

3. ¿Luis está comiendo un sándwich?

_____

4. ¿Pablo está leyendo un libro?

_____

5. ¿El abuelo está escuchando la radio?

_____

6. ¿El perro está durmiendo en la cocina?

_____

5-19   ¿Qué está haciendo su familia? Can you guess what your own family members are doing at this moment? Write a paragraph of three to five sentences about what the members of your family might be doing right now.

_____

_____

_____

_____

_____

_____

_____

Nombre: _____   **Fecha:** _____

2. Describing physical and emotional states: Expressions with *tener*
(Textbook p. 167)

5-20   ¿Qué tienen? Give the expression with *tener* that describes each of the pictures below.

1. _____

2. _____

3. _____

4. _____

5. _____

6. _____

5-21   Adriana y sus amigos. Read about the situations of Adriana and her friends and select the answer that indicates how they feel.

1. Adriana trabaja mucho y duerme muy poco. Por eso siempre...

    a. tiene suerte.   **b.** tiene sueño.   **c.** tiene razón.

2. Jaime juega al tenis los sábados por la mañana. Después de jugar, toma refrescos porque...

    a. tiene frío.   **b.** tiene miedo.   **c.** tiene sed.

3. Adriana y Alicia están a dieta. Sólo toman jugo para el desayuno y comen vegetales y frutas para el almuerzo. A la hora de la cena ellas...

    a. tienen hambre.   **b.** tienen prisa.   **c.** tienen calor.

4. Adriana y su hermana Amanda siempre juegan a la lotería, y nunca ganan (*win*). Ellas no...

    a. tienen cuidado.   **b.** tienen suerte.   **c.** tienen razón.

5. La clase de español empieza a las ocho de la mañana. Son las ocho menos diez, y Adriana está todavía (*still*) en la cafetería. No puede hablar con Jaime porque ella...

    a. tiene frío.   **b.** tiene sed.   **c.** tiene prisa.

5-22   Y ahora, ¿qué tienen? Listen to the descriptions of Adriana and her friends and family. Choose the best expression with **tener** and write a complete sentence to describe them.

MODELO: You hear: Adriana está corriendo en el parque y quiere beber agua.

   You write: Adriana *tiene sed*.

1. Adriana _____.

2. Alicia _____.

3. Los niños _____.

4. Jaime _____.

5. El abuelo _____.

5-23 **La familia del profesor Rivera.** Look at the pictures of Professor Rivera and his family and write an expression using **tener** to describe each one.

1. El profesor Rivera _____.

2. La señora Rivera _____.

3. Susanita Rivera _____.

5-24   ¿Qué hace usted? What do you do when you have certain feelings and emotions? Read the questions below and explain orally what you usually do in each situation.

MODELO: You see: ¿Qué hace usted cuando tiene hambre?

You say: *Cuando tengo hambre, como una hamburguesa.*

1. ¿Qué hace usted cuando tiene sed?

2. ¿Qué hace usted cuando tiene sueño?

3. ¿Qué hace usted cuando tiene frío?

4. ¿Qué hace usted cuando tiene calor?

3. Avoiding repetition in speaking and writing: Direct object nouns and pronouns (Textbook p. 170)

5-25   ¿Qué quieren hacer? Read the following sentences about what Adriana and her friends want to do, and replace the direct object noun with the appropriate pronoun.

MODELO: Adriana quiere preparar el pastel.

Lo quiere preparar.

1. Adriana quiere hacer las camas.

    _____ quiere hacer.

2. Adriana quiere comprar los libros.

    _____ quiere comprar.

3. Alicia quiere sacar una buena nota en la clase de español.

    _____ quiere sacar.

4. Jaime quiere preparar la cena.

    _____ quiere preparar.

5. Yo quiero tomar café con leche.

    _____ quiero tomar.

6. Adriana y Alicia quieren limpiar el apartamento.

    _____ quieren limpiar.

7. Jaime quiere regar las plantas.

    _____ quiere regar.

5-26   La primera fiesta. Adriana and Alicia are planning a housewarming party in their new apartment and they are talking about what needs to be done. Read the statements and questions below. Then listen to the responses and match each response with the statement that correctly precedes it.

_____ 1. Primero, el apartamento está sucio.

_____ 2. Además la cocina está muy desordenada.

_____ 3. ¿Y para tomar? Tenemos que comprar unos refrescos…

_____ 4. Muy bien… y ¿por qué no ponemos unas flores en la sala?

_____ 5. Otra cosa importante: tenemos que llamar a nuestros amigos.

5-27   Preparando la fiesta. Adriana is talking about what still needs to be done for the housewarming party.

1. **a.** el pan	**b.** la ensalada	**c.** los refrescos	**d.** las flores
2. **a.** el baño	**b.** la cocina	**c.** los cuartos	**d.** las mesas
3. **a.** el coche	**b.** la fruta	**c.** los platos	**d.** las sábanas
4. **a.** a Luis	**b.** a Linda	**c.** a Lisa y Óscar	**d.** a Mirta y Ana
5. **a.** el teléfono	**b.** la mesa	**c.** los discos	**d.** las sillas

5-28   La perfecta anfitriona (*hostess*). The guests have finally arrived. Listen to their questions and select the appropriate answer.

1. **a.** Claro que puedes tomarlo.   **c.** Claro que puedes tomarlos.
   b. Claro que puedes tomarla.   **d.** Claro que puedes tomarlas.

2. **a.** Sí, pueden usarlo.   **c.** Sí, pueden usarlos.
   b. Sí, pueden usarla.   **d.** Sí, pueden usarlas.

3. **a.** Lo tenemos en la cocina.   **c.** Los tenemos en la cocina.
   b. La tenemos en la cocina.   **d.** Las tenemos en la cocina.

4. **a.** Sí, están junto a la puerta; ¿lo ves?   **c.** Sí, están junto a la puerta; ¿los ves?
   b. Sí, están junto a la puerta; ¿la ves?   **d.** Sí, están junto a la puerta; ¿las ves?

5. **a.** Lo está tocando Tomás.   **c.** Los está tocando Tomás.
   b. La está tocando Tomás.   **d.** Las está tocando Tomás.

5-29 Al día siguiente. The party turned out great and everyone had fun! Now it is time to clean up, so you have offered to help. Answer Adriana's and Alicia's questions affirmatively, and give your responses orally. Be sure to use the correct pronouns in your answers.

MODELO: You hear: ¿Vamos a limpiar el apartamento?

You say: *Sí, lo vamos a limpiar.*

1. ...

2. ...

3. ...

4. ...

5. ...

6. ...

7. ...

5-30 Las opiniones de Adriana. Read the following paragraph, in which Adriana explains how she feels about several people. Write down her attitude toward each person or persons.

Hay muchas personas importantes en mi vida. Quiero mucho a mis padres; son personas muy especiales. También aprecio mucho a mis abuelos. Ellos siempre vienen de visita durante las vacaciones. Además, tengo una buena relación con mi hermana, Amanda. Mi hermana y yo tenemos intereses similares, así que la comprendo muy bien a ella. Mis amigas son maravillosas. Finalmente, me gustan mis clases y respeto mucho a mis profesores.

MODELO: su padre: *A su padre lo quiere mucho.*

1. su madre: _____

2. sus abuelos: _____

3. su hermana: _____

4. sus profesores: _____

5-31   La familia de Alicia. Now read the following paragraph about Alicia's family and locate the five direct object pronouns. Then write the person or persons to whom the direct object pronoun refers.

Mi familia es muy interesante. Mi madre trabaja en un banco y después va a casa para limpiar. La[1] respeto y admiro mucho porque trabaja muy duro (*hard*). Además, es muy cariñosa. Mi padre también es muy cariñoso. Mi hermano y yo siempre reñimos (*fight*), pero lo[2] quiero mucho. Tengo dos hermanas gemelas; tenemos una buena relación y las[3] quiero mucho. Mis abuelos viven lejos, pero los[4] visito una vez al año durante las vacaciones. Mi tía Margarita es soltera, y aunque tiene 40 años, vive con mis abuelos. Mi tía quiere mucho a mi abuela y siempre la[5] ayuda con las tareas domésticas.

1. _____

2. _____

3. _____

4. _____

5. _____

4. Pointing out and identifying people and things: Demonstrative adjectives and pronouns (Textbook p. 175)

5-32   ¿Dónde quiere los muebles? You are spending two weeks at the home of Alicia's family and her mother has bought a few new things for her home. Complete her mother's conversation with the delivery man with the correct demonstrative adjectives.

EMPLEADO: ¿Dónde quiere (1) _____ espejo que tengo aquí?

SRA. RUIZ: En (2) _____ dormitorio de allá.

EMPLEADO: Y ¿dónde pongo (3) _____ lámparas que están ahí?

SRA. RUIZ: La lámpara blanca va aquí, y las otras dos en (4) _____ habitación pequeña de ahí.

EMPLEADO: ¿Y (5) _____ cuadros que están aquí?

SRA. RUIZ: (6) _____ cuadro de ahí va detrás del sofá.

EMPLEADO: ¿Y (7) _____ otro que tengo en mis manos?

SRA. RUIZ: (8) _____ otro va en el comedor.

5-33 ¿Qué es esto? You were not able to do a lot of shopping on your trip, so when you return you visit a local Nicaraguan store. You are not familiar with all of the items, so you ask some questions. Complete the following conversation with the salesman using **esto, eso,** or **aquello.**

USTED: ¿Qué es (1) _____ que está ahí al lado suyo (*your side*)?

VENDEDOR: ¿(2) _____ ? Es un molinillo (*little grinder*). Lo usamos para moler (*grind*) el chocolate o el "tiste", una bebida de maíz y cacao.

USTED: ¿Y (3) _____ que está allá? ¿Qué es?

VENDEDOR: Es un "guacal". Es una calabaza seca (*dry gourd*), y la usamos para servir la comida. Y también usamos unos pequeños para servir bebidas.

USTED: ¿Y (4) _____ que está aquí?

VENDEDOR: (5) _____ es una "maraca", un instrumento musical. Usamos dos, una en cada mano, y con ellas seguimos el ritmo de la música.

5-34 De compras. Now that you have some Nicaraguan items, you realize that you need a few more things. Complete the questions you are going to ask the store attendant with the correct demonstrative adjectives.

1. Ves un reloj en la pared (*wall*). El dependiente está un poco lejos, pero te acercas (*get near to*) dónde está él y le preguntas: ¿Cuánto cuesta _____ reloj?

2. El dependiente tiene una guitarra en la mano. Tú le preguntas: ¿Cuánto cuesta _____ guitarra?

3. Tu amiga te muestra (*shows*) unos discos compactos que te gustan mucho, y le preguntas al dependiente: ¿Cuánto cuestan _____ discos compactos?

4. También ves unas películas al otro lado de la tienda. Se las señalas (*You point them out*) al dependiente, que está a tu lado, y preguntas: ¿Cuánto cuestan _____ películas de ahí?

5. Tu amiga tiene un mapa en la mano, y tú lo necesitas para la clase de geografía. Le preguntas al dependiente: ¿Cuánto cuesta _____ mapa?

5-35   Más cosas para el apartamento. You now have some furniture, but you are still looking for a few items for the new apartment. Adriana and Alicia offer some suggestions; unfortunately, you do not have the same taste. Listen to their suggestions and choose an appropriate response.

1. Sí, pero yo prefiero _____.

   a. este   **b.** esta   **c.** estos   **d.** estas

2. Sí, pero a mí me gusta _____.

   a. ese   **b.** esa   **c.** esos   **d.** esas

3. Sí pero _____ son mejores (*better*).

   a. aquel   **b.** aquella   **c.** aquellos   **d.** aquellas

4. Sí, pero quiero _____.

   a. este   **b.** esta   **c.** estos   **d.** estas

5. Sí, pero _____ son mejores.

   a. este   **b.** esta   **c.** estos   **d.** estas

MOSAICOS

A escuchar

Antes de escuchar

5-36   Nuevos vecinos. Your new neighbors seem to be busy cleaning their house. Before you listen, create a mental image of all the rooms in the house and the things that might need to be cleaned. Now, make one list of rooms and another list of the chores that your neighbors might be doing.

CUARTOS

_____

_____

_____

_____

_____

TAREAS DOMÉSTICAS

_____

_____

_____

_____

_____

Escuchar

5-37   Una reunión familiar. Listen to the following passage once for the general idea: why are the neighbors cleaning? Then listen again, paying more attention to the details of what each person is doing. Finally, indicate whether each statement is **Cierto** or **Falso**.

1. Los abuelos van a llegar esta tarde.	Cierto	Falso
2. Los tíos están ayudando a la familia.	Cierto	Falso
3. El padre está bañando al perro.	Cierto	Falso
4. La mamá y su hija están poniendo la mesa.	Cierto	Falso
5. Toda la familia está muy contenta por la visita de los abuelos.	Cierto	Falso

Después de escuchar

5-38   ¿Qué más tienen que hacer? Did your new neighbors forget to do anything? Check over the list you made in activity **5-36** and compare that list with the information in activity **5-37**. Write down any other chores you thought of that your neighbors need to do before their family members arrive.

_____

_____

_____

_____

A conversar

5-39   Ahora usted. You become acquainted with some new friends of Adriana's. Tell them about where you live: whether it is a house or an apartment, the different rooms it has, the furniture and other items in it, and the household chores that you do. Do you like your current home? Why or why not?

A leer

Antes de leer

5-40   El artículo. Look at the title of the following article. Before you read the article, review the following list of activities. If the activity listed is a household chore, select **Sí**; if it is not, select **No**.

1. ganar dinero	Sí	No		**5.** planchar la ropa	Sí	No
2. trabajar fuera de casa	Sí	No		**6.** quedarse en casa	Sí	No
3. limpiar	Sí	No		**7.** casarse	Sí	No
4. barrer	Sí	No		**8.** cocinar	Sí	No

Leer

5-41   ¿Quién es el responsable? Read the following article and then indicate whether the statements that follow are **Cierto** or **Falso**.

¿Quién es el responsable de las tareas domésticas?

Las amas de casa (*homemakers*) realizan cada día una labor de trabajo inmensa, pero no reciben un salario por su trabajo. En muchos casos el trabajo de estas mujeres pasa desapercibido (*unnoticed*), y ellas no reciben ni el agradecimiento (*gratitude*) de sus familias.

Aunque (*Although*) es cierto que en los últimos (*last*) años hay un aumento de mujeres en las diferentes áreas del mundo laboral —la industria, el comercio, e incluso (*even*) en la política— y como es natural reciben un salario por su trabajo, muchas mujeres todavía se dedican a los quehaceres del hogar como limpiar la casa, lavar, planchar la ropa, coser (*sew*), y cuidar a los hijos.

El gran problema para las mujeres que trabajan en casa persiste; no reciben ni salario ni recompensa (*compensation*) por las interminables horas de dedicación al hogar, y en muchas familias el hombre no participa en las tareas domésticas. Un estudio reciente revela que cuando una mujer se casa, el tiempo que pasa en las tareas domésticas aumenta (*goes up*) siete horas. Al contrario, cuando se casa un hombre, el tiempo que pasa en las tareas domésticas disminuye (*goes down*) una hora. Esta práctica es totalmente injusta; o las mujeres deben recibir un salario por su trabajo en la casa o deben recibir la ayuda del esposo. Por eso, antes del matrimonio, los esposos deben ponerse de acuerdo en las responsabilidades domésticas de cada uno.

Todos en el hogar deben ser responsables de las tareas domésticas. Así la vida es más fácil y justa.

---

1. Las mujeres reciben un salario por su trabajo en casa.	Cierto	Falso
2. Muchos hombres trabajan para ganar dinero para sustentar *(support)* a la familia.	Cierto	Falso
3. La mujer trabaja más en casa que el hombre.	Cierto	Falso
4. Cuando un hombre se casa, el tiempo que pasa en las tareas domésticas aumenta.	Cierto	Falso
5. Las tareas domésticas deben ser la obligación de todos.	Cierto	Falso

Después de leer

5-42 ¿Qué opina usted? Consider your opinions on the division of labor in the home. Do you believe stay-at-home wives and mothers should receive compensation for their work? Should men and children also participate in household chores? Write a paragraph in Spanish explaining your ideas.

_____

_____

_____

_____

_____

_____

A escribir

Antes de escribir

5-43 Preparación. Think of your own household. Who takes care of the following chores? Write your answers on the lines below, using the choices in the word bank.

Mamá   Papá   un/a hermano/a   otra persona   usted

1. cocinar _____
2. comprar la comida _____
3. limpiar la casa _____
4. lavar la ropa _____
5. planchar la ropa _____
6. hacer las camas _____
7. poner la mesa _____
8. lavar los platos _____
9. sacar la basura _____
10. cortar el césped _____

Escribir

5-44 Su experiencia. The author of the article in activity **5-41** has her own blog, where people are discussing their personal situations with regard to household chores. Write a post and tell her about your own family experience. Remember to mention the following information:

- how the work is divided in your home
- which chores are done in your house, and how often
- how your home compares to that of the families described in the article

_____

_____

_____

_____

_____

_____

_____

Después de escribir

5-45 Revisión. Ask your instructor or one of your classmates to read your blog post in activity **5-44** and give you comments. Then read what you have written and check carefully for correct tone, vocabulary and spelling. Make sure you have included direct object pronouns, when possible, to avoid repetition. Finally, rewrite it with the corrections you have made.

_____

_____

_____

_____

_____

_____

_____

ENFOQUE CULTURAL

5-46   Lectura y comprensión. Reread the *Enfoque cultural* section on pages 184–185 of your textbook and then indicate whether each statement is **Cierto** or **Falso**.

1. Una característica de Centroamérica es la gran cantidad de volcanes.

   Cierto   Falso

2. Los volcanes de Centroamérica ya no están activos.

   Cierto   Falso

3. El Volcán de Cerro Negro es el más viejo de la región.

   Cierto   Falso

4. Los científicos se preocupan cuando la actividad normal de los volcanes aumenta.

   Cierto   Falso

5. La capital de Nicaragua es San Cristóbal.

   Cierto   Falso

6. Los terremotos son frecuentes en Centroamérica.

   Cierto   Falso

7. En 2001, murieron más de mil personas a causa de los terremotos.

   Cierto   Falso

8. En Centroamérica, las playas y las selvas son espectaculares.

   Cierto   Falso

9. En Honduras hay muchas montañas, pero no hay selvas.

   Cierto   Falso

10. Hay muchas especies diferentes de plantas y animales en Honduras.

    Cierto   Falso

5-47   Buscando casa. Visit the *Mosaicos* webpage to look at classified ads in each of the countries studied in this chapter. Write down the information for your favorite house or apartment in each one of the countries in the spaces provided below.

1. país: Nicaragua

   barrio y/o dirección: _____

   descripción de apartamento o casa: _____

   tamaño (opcional): _____

   precio (en córdobas o en dólares): _____

   contacto (número de teléfono o correo electrónico): _____

2. país: El Salvador

   barrio y/o dirección: _____

   descripción de apartamento o casa: _____

   tamaño (opcional): _____

   precio (en colones o en dólares): _____

   contacto (número de teléfono o correo electrónico): _____

3. país: Honduras

   barrio y/o dirección: _____

   descripción del apartamento o casa: _____

   tamaño (opcional): _____

   precio (en lempiras o en dólares): _____

   contacto (número de teléfono o correo electrónico): _____

REPASO

5-48 El apartamento de Adriana y Alicia. Adriana and Alicia have rented an apartment together for the school year. Unfortunately, the apartment is not equipped with furniture or appliances. Help the girls make a list by indicating some of the things they need to buy for the house.

aparatos eléctricos para la cocina:

_____

_____

_____

muebles para la sala:

_____

_____

muebles y accesorios para los dormitorios:

_____

_____

_____

muebles para el comedor:

_____

_____

5-49   Ordenando la casa. Adriana has just sent you an instant message asking you to go out to lunch. Unfortunately, your house and your yard are a mess and your parents are coming to visit. You are very busy cleaning and getting ready. Write Adriana a brief e-mail response, and be sure to include the following information:

- a response to her invitation

- an explanation for the mess in your house and yard

- the chores you are doing (present progressive) to get everything ready

| |
| |
| |
| |
| |
| |
| |
| |
| |
| |

5-50   La fiesta de cumpleaños. Adriana is talking with Jaime on the phone about a surprise birthday party she is throwing for Alicia. Look at the pictures below and then listen to their conversation. Choose **Sí** if the information represented in the image is mentioned in the conversation and **No** if it is not mentioned.

1. Sí   No

2. Sí   No

3. Si   No   **4.** Si   No

5-51   Una casa nueva. Jaime and his roommate Mateo have also rented a house for the school year. Read the description of their house and the statements that follow. Finally, indicate whether each statement is **Cierto, Falso** or **No dice** (not mentioned in the passage).

La casa de Mateo y Jaime es bastante grande; tiene dos dormitorios y dos baños completos. Ellos están contentos porque cada uno va a tener su propio baño. Además, Mateo está feliz porque la casa tiene una cocina muy moderna. Eso es muy importante porque él cocina todos los días. En la cocina hay un microondas y una estufa con un horno eléctrico. Jaime está contento porque normalmente limpia la cocina después de comer, y hay un lavaplatos nuevo. Todos los cuartos de la casa son grandes. También hay un jardín donde el perro que tienen los chicos puede pasar el día. La casa no está lejos de la universidad; los compañeros de cuarto pueden caminar a clase en 20 minutos o tomar el autobús que pasa por su casa cada media hora.

1. Mateo y Jaime son compañeros de cuarto.	Cierto	Falso	No dice
2. La casa que tienen no es muy grande, pero hay dos dormitorios y dos baños.	Cierto	Falso	No dice
3. Jaime y Mateo estudian en la cocina.	Cierto	Falso	No dice
4. Jaime prefiere cocinar, y también lava los platos.	Cierto	Falso	No dice
5. Hay un jardín para el perro.	Cierto	Falso	No dice
6. Hay una piscina en el jardín.	Cierto	Falso	No dice
7. Los chicos pueden tomar el autobús a clase.	Cierto	Falso	No dice

APPENDIX

Stress and written accents in Spanish

Rules for Written Accents

The following rules are based on pronunciation.

1. If a word ends in *n*, *s*, or a vowel, the penultimate (second-to-last) syllable is usually stressed.

   Examples: caminan

   muchos

   silla

2. If a word ends in a consonant other than *n* or *s*, the last syllable is stressed.

   Example: fa**tal**

3. Words that are exceptions to the preceding rules have an accent mark on the stressed vowel.

   Examples: sar**tén**

   lápices

   ma**má**

   fácil

4. **Separation of diphthongs:** When *i* or *u* are combined with another vowel, they are pronounced as one sound (a diphthong). When each vowel sound is pronounced separately, a written accent mark is placed over the stressed vowel (either the *i* or the *u*).

   Example: gracias **dí**a

Because the written accents in the following examples are not determined by pronunciation, the accent mark must be memorized as part of the spelling of the words as they are learned.

5. **Homonyms.** When two words are spelled the same, but have different meanings, a written accent is used to distinguish and differentiate meaning.

	Examples:	**de**	*of*	**dé**	*give* (formal command)
		el	*the*	**él**	*he*
		mas	*but*	**más**	*more*
		mi	my	**mí**	me
		se	*him/herself, (to) him/her/them*	**sé**	*I know, be* (formal command)
		si	*if*	**sí**	*yes*
		te	*(to) you*	**té**	*tea*
		tu	*your*	**tú**	*you*

6. **Interrogatives and Exclamations:** In questions (direct and indirect) and exclamations, a written accent is placed over the following words: **dónde, cómo, cuándo, cuál(es), quién(es), cuánto(s)/cuánta(s),** and **qué.**

PRÁCTICA

Activity 1 (Capítulo 1)

Read the following words and rewrite each one, placing the correct accent mark(s) accordingly.

1. tambien _____

2. facil _____

3. dificil _____

4. economia _____

5. ciencias politicas _____

6. antropologia _____

Activity 2 (Capítulo 1)

Read the following questions and locate the word or words that require a written accent. Then write each word in the order it appears in the question, and place the correct accent mark(s) accordingly.

¿Donde miras la television?

1. _____

2. _____

¿Que compras en la libreria?

3. _____

4. _____

¿Donde estudias normalmente?

5. _____

¿Donde esta Maria?

6. _____

7. _____

8. _____

¿A que hora es la clase de español?

9. _____

Activity 3 (Capítulo 2)

Read the following words, and then complete each one with the correct accented letter.

1. caf __
2. portugu__s
3. japon__s
4. simp__tico
5. d__bil
6. antip___tico

Activity 4 (Capítulo 2)

Read the following ad that Pablo wrote in order to find a pen pal with common interests. Locate each word that is missing an accent mark; then rewrite the words in the order they appear, placing the correct accent marks accordingly.

Me llamo Pablo Sosa. Tengo 31 años, y soy chileno. Soy agradable y muy trabajador. Me gusta hacer mi trabajo a la perfeccion, pero soy tolerante. Mi pasion son los autos convertibles. Deseo mantener correspondencia por correo electronico con jovenes del extranjero para intercambiar informacion sobre los convertibles europeos y americanos.

1. _____   4. _____
2. _____   5. _____
3. _____

⮞)) Activity 5 (Capítulo 3)

Listen to the pronunciation of each of the following words and select the syllable that should be accented, according to the rules.

1. can cion
2. mu si ca
3. re u nion
4. pe li cu la
5. ja mon
6. sand wich
7. pe rio di co
8. pa is

Activity 6 (Capítulo 3)

Read the following paragraph about fast food. Locate each word that is missing an accent mark; then rewrite the words in the order they appear, placing the correct accent marks accordingly.

La comida rapida es muy popular entre la gente joven. Las "hamburgueserias" de tipo norteamericano existen en muchas ciudades del mundo hispano. Los restaurantes de este tipo en los paises hispanos frecuentemente combinan comida de Estados Unidos con comidas tipicas de su pais.

1. _____   4. _____

2. _____   5. _____

3. _____

Activity 7 (Capítulo 4)

Read the following words and rewrite each with the appropriate accent mark.

1. tio _____   4. papa _____

2. tia _____   5. mama _____

3. fotografia _____

Activity 8 (Capítulo 4)

Read the following description of a Colombian family. Choose the correct word (accented or unaccented) according the rules that you have learned.

Reminder: A Spanish word can only have one written accent. Therefore, an adjective with a written accent loses the regular accent when –ísimo is added.

Example: fácil – facilísimo.

Mi [(1) mama/mamá] tiene un hermano, mi [(2) tío/tío] Raul. Su esposa es mi [(3) tia/tía] Laura. Tienen tres hijos, y ellos viven [(4) tambien/también] en [(5) Bogota/Bogotá]. Mi primo [(6) Rafael/Rafáel] es el menor. Mis [(7) primas/prímas] Sandra y Sara son gemelas. Mis primos son [(8) simpatiquisimos/simpatiquísimos] y pasamos mucho [(9) tiempo/tiémpo] juntos.

Mis [(10) tios/tíos] tienen dos [(11) sobrinos/sobrínos] en [(12) Bogota/Bogotá], mi hermana [(13) Ines/Inés] y yo. Su otra [(14) sobrina/sobrína], la hija de mi [(15) tia/tía] Lola, vive en Cartagena, al norte del [(16) pais/país].

Activity 9 (Capítulo 5)

Rewrite the following words, placing the written accent on the correct vowel.

1. arbol _____
2. jardin _____
3. jabon _____
4. sabana _____

5. comoda _____
6. lavanderia _____
7. calefaccion _____

Activity 10 (Capítulo 5)

Choose the appropriate vowels (accented or unaccented) to complete the words in the sentences below.

1. Est__ cas__ de dos p__sos est__ en una c__udad. Tiene muchas ventanas en cada piso, p__ro no tiene jard__n.

2. Aquella casa d__nde est__n la madre y su hij__ es de material s__lido y de un color alegre.

3. Esa casa es de construcci__n s__lida y ti__ne dos pisos y un gar__je. Tiene una pequeña __rea verde en frente.

Activity 11 (Capítulo 6)

Rewrite the following words or phrases, placing the written accent on the correct vowel.

1. Me gustaria _____
2. artesania _____
3. sueter _____
4. sosten _____

5. camison _____
6. poliester _____
7. algodon _____
8. almacen _____

Activity 12 (Capítulo 6)

Listen to the following paragraph and choose the appropriately accented word according to what you hear.

Reminder: The preterit form requires an accent mark on the first and third person singular.

Examples: Yo hablé. El habló.

La semana pasada, yo [(1) compré/cómpre] un hermoso vestido de fiesta. Roberto [(2) cómpro/compró] un traje, una camisa y zapatos. La ceremonia religiosa fue a las 7:00 de la tarde. La fiesta con familia y amigos [(3) empézo/empezó] a las 9:00 y [(4) término/terminó] a las 4:00 de la mañana. Todos comimos y bailamos mucho.

Activity 13 (Capítulo 7)

Read the words below and complete each one with the appropriate accented vowel.

1. atm___sfera
2. ___rbitro
3. f___tbol
4. esqu___
5. b___isbol

Activity 14 (Capítulo 7)

Listen to the following paragraph about sports. Rewrite the words in bold with the missing accent mark, or as they appear if no accent mark is necessary.

Entre las grandes **pasiones** nacionales, desde luego, **esta** el **futbol**. Desde su **infancia**, muchos uruguayos acompañan fielmente (*faithfully*) a sus **equipos** favoritos. En varias ocasiones, la **seleccion** nacional uruguaya **gano titulos** y campeonatos importantes.

Pero los **uruguayos** son un pueblo inquieto, de una personalidad **versatil** que no limita su **interes** a un solo deporte. El **basquetbol**, el ciclismo, el rugby, el boxeo y la **pelota** de mano son otros deportes que tienen muchos aficionados.

1. _____
2. _____
3. _____
4. _____
5. _____
6. _____
7. _____

8. _____
9. _____
10. _____
11. _____
12. _____
13. _____

Activity 15 (Capítulo 8)

Read the words and phrases below and rewrite them with the appropriate accent mark.

1. ultimo _____
2. hoy en dia _____
3. melodia _____
4. tradicion _____

5. procesion _____
6. invitacion _____
7. alegria _____

Activity 16 (Capítulo 8)

Read the paragraph below and choose the correct word (accented or unaccented) according to the rules you have learned.

Era el cumpleaños de nuestra gran [(1) amiga/amíga] Guadalupe [(2) Martinez/Martínez]. Aunque [(3) tenia/tenía] solo veinte años, Guadalupe [(4)era/éra] una chica excepcional. [(5) Estudiaba/Estudíaba] en la UNAM y [(6) tambien/también] trabajaba para ayudar a su familia de ocho [(7) hermanos/hermános]. Todos sus amigos la [(8) admirabamos/admirábamos] por su generosidad, optimismo y [(9) alegria/alegría]. Guadalupe era la amiga que todos [(10) soñabamos/soñábamos] tener.

Activity 17 (Capítulo 9)

Listen as the words below are pronounced and rewrite each word with the appropriate accent mark.

1. curriculum _____
2. peluqueria _____
3. compania _____
4. policia _____

5. medico _____
6. interprete _____
7. cientifico _____

Activity 18 (Capítulo 9)

Read the conversation below and find the words that require a written accent. Write the words, in the order they appear, with the appropriate accent mark.

Reminders:
Homonyms are distinguished by the use of an accent mark. Example: sí vs. si.

Accent marks are sometimes required when pronouns are added to commands, gerunds and infinitives. Example: Dámelo.

Buenos dias, señorita. Me llamo Ricardo Roldan Diaz. ¿Podria darme una solicitud para el puesto de asistente de contador?

Claro que si, Sr. Roldan. Por favor, llene la solicitud y mandenosla pronto.

¿Puedo mandarsela por correo electronico?

Si, pero enviela tambien por correo postal.

1. _____
2. _____
3. _____
4. _____
5. _____
6. _____

7. _____
8. _____
9. _____
10. _____
11. _____
12. _____

Activity 19 (Capítulo 10)

Read the words below and select the word with the correct accented vowel.

1. todavía   todávia
2. lácteo   lactéo
3. fréir   freír

4. mélon   melón
5. limón   límon
6. azúcar   ázucar

Activity 20 (Capítulo 10)

Listen to the following paragraph and complete it by choosing the correct accented or unaccented words.

La comida de los [(1) paises/países] hispanoamericanos es muy [(2) variada/varíada]. En Ecuador, igual que en [(3) Peru/Perú], el [(4) ceviche/ceviché] de pescado o de [(5) camaron/camarón] es muy popular. Otro de los platos [(6) más/mas] populares es la fritada, que combina diversas carnes con [(7) platano/plátano] maduro, el tostado y [(8) maiz/maíz]. Entre los postres, [(9) ademas/además] de la [(10) pasteleria/pastelería], es el muy sabroso [(11) dulce/dulcé] de higos.

Activity 21 (Capítulo 11)

Listen to the words below and rewrite each word with the appropriate accent mark.

1. inyeccion   _____
2. antibiotico   _____
3. farmaceutico   _____
4. clinica   _____
5. tension   _____
6. sintoma   _____
7. infeccion   _____

8. cancer   _____
9. pulmon   _____
10. oido   _____
11. musculo   _____
12. estomago   _____
13. corazon   _____

Activity 22 (Capítulo 11)

Choose the appropriate vowel (accented or unaccented) to complete the words in each sentence below.

1. Los res__dentes del barr__o prefieren que la cl__nica no cierre antes de las s__ete.
2. La niñ__ espera que el enf__rmero no le ponga una inyecci__n.
3. Ojal__ que puedas llevarme a la cit__ con la m__dica.
4. El m__dico le proh__be que s__lga por unos d__as.

Activity 23 (Capítulo 12)

Read the words below and complete each one with the appropriate accented vowel.

1. cajero autom__tico
2. correo electr__nico
3. buz__n
4. linea a__rea
5. avi__n
6. autob__s

Activity 24 (Capítulo 12)

Read the dialogue. Then, rewrite the words that appear in bold, and include a written accent when appropriate.

–**Jose** Luis, mi maleta casi **esta** lista. ¿Y la tuya?

–¡La **mia** no! **Despues** del programa la voy a empacar. ¿Ya empacaste tus libros, **mama**?

–Los **mios** ya **estan** en **mi maletin**. ¿Y los **zapatos** de Nora?

–Los **suyos estan** en su mochila.

1. _____
2. _____
3. _____
4. _____
5. _____
6. _____
7. _____
8. _____
9. _____
10. _____
11. _____
12. _____
13. _____

Activity 25 (Capítulo 13)

Listen as the words and phrases below are pronounced, and rewrite them with the appropriate accent marks.

1. bailarin _____
2. politica _____
3. poblacion _____
4. a traves de _____
5. area _____
6. exito _____
7. segun _____

Activity 26 (Capítulo 13)

Read the sentences below. Rewrite the words that appear in bold and include the appropriate written accent for those words that require one.

¿Que haria usted?

Compraria boletos rapidamente para no perder la oportunidad de verla.

Visitaria las salas donde estan las pinturas de Velazquez.

Compraria una novela de Gabriel Garcia Marquez.

1. _____
2. _____
3. _____
4. _____
5. _____
6. _____
7. _____

8. _____
9. _____
10. _____
11. _____
12. _____
13. _____
14. _____

Activity 27 (Capítulo 14)

Choose the word with the correct written accent.

1. enérgico   energíco
2. mayória   mayoría
3. estádistica   estadística
4. separacíon   separación

Activity 28 (Capítulo 14)

Listen to the following sentences and choose the correct form of the words given.

Cuando yo [(1) tenia/tenía] diez años, ya [(2) habia/había] escuchado [(3) discusiones/discusiónes] [(4) politicas/políticas] en mi casa.

Cuando yo [(5) tenia/tenía] [(6) dieciseis/dieciséis] años, mis amigos y yo nos [(7) habiamos/habíamos] [(8) inscrito/inscritó] en un partido [(9) politico/político].

Cuando [(10) paso/pasó] el primer [(11) semestre/seméstre] de la universidad, yo ya me [(12) habia/había] acostumbrado a lo que [(13) tenia/tenía] que hacer.

Activity 29 (Capítulo 15)

Read the words below and select the word with the correct accented vowel.

1. paracaídas   paracáidas
2. preservacíon   preservación
3. deforestacíon   deforestación
4. pérdida   perdída
5. ráton   ratón
6. cárton   cartón
7. pórtatil   portátil

Activity 30 (Capítulo 15)

Read the sentences below and find the words that require a written accent. Write the words, in the order you find them, with the appropriate accent mark.

Si tuvieramos mucho dinero, comprariamos una casa.

Si hubiera tiempo suficiente, estudiaria el italiano.

Si fueramos a Disneylandia, me subiria a Splash Mountain tres veces.

La atmosfera sufrira un calentamiento que hara subir el nivel del mar.

Habran robots que se ocuparan de hacer la limpieza.

1. _____
2. _____
3. _____
4. _____
5. _____
6. _____
7. _____
8. _____
9. _____
10. _____

Notas

Notas

Notas

Notas

Notas

Notas

Notas

Notas